THE QUILTER'S PRACTICAL GUIDE TO
COLOR

BECKY GOLDSMITH

**Includes 10
Skill-Building
Projects**

C&T PUBLISHING

Text, photography, and artwork copyright © 2015 by Becky Goldsmith

Photography and artwork copyright © 2015 by C&T Publishing, Inc.

PUBLISHER: Amy Marson

CREATIVE DIRECTOR: Gailen Runge

ART DIRECTOR: Kristy Zacharias

EDITORS: Lynn Koolish and Katie Van Amburg

TECHNICAL EDITORS: Debbie Rodgers and Gailen Runge

COVER/BOOK DESIGNER: April Mostek

PRODUCTION COORDINATOR: Freesia Pearson Blizard

PRODUCTION EDITOR: Alice Mace Nakanishi

ILLUSTRATORS: Becky Goldsmith and Kerry Graham

PHOTO ASSISTANT: Mary Peyton Peppo

INSTRUCTIONAL PHOTOGRAPHY by Diane Pedersen, unless otherwise noted

Published by C&T Publishing, Inc., P.O. Box 1456, Lafayette, CA 94549

Library of Congress Cataloging-in-Publication Data

Goldsmith, Becky, 1956-

  The quilter's practical guide to color : includes 10 skill-building projects / Becky Goldsmith.

    pages cm

ISBN 978-1-60705-864-9

1. Quilting. 2. Color in textile crafts. 3. Quilting--Patterns. 4. Quilts. I. Title.

TT835.G332465 2015

746.46--dc23

                    2014028562

Printed in China

10 9 8 7 6 5 4 3 2 1

DEDICATION

I dedicate this book to my family and to Linda and Paul Jenkins, who feel like family. They all do more than love me—they put up with me.

My husband, Steve, deserves special attention. He takes such good care of me in a variety of ways. Rather than bringing home flowers and jewelry, he quietly makes sure that things happen. The car always has gas, the trash never overflows, and (more important) it is he who puts dinner on the table every night. Best of all, when he looks at me, I know that he loves me. I wouldn't be the same "me" without him beside me.

Guess what else? Steve also bastes my quilts, and after they are quilted, he hand stitches the bindings on my quilts. I do love this man.

Steve basting *Tick Tock* (page 98)

ACKNOWLEDGMENTS

My heartfelt thanks go to Linda Jenkins, my friend and business partner, who for many years has patiently let me know both when I get it right *and* when I don't.

My daughter-in-law, Lorna, did so much to make this book possible. She has taken over much of the business end of pieceocake.com. Thanks to her dedication, I found the time to write this book and make the quilts.

I thank Roberta Horton for all she taught me through her books and in classes—and especially for her book *Scrap Quilts: The Art of Making Do*. I learned so much from that book 30 years ago. Upon re-reading, I learned even more.

And I must thank Lynn Koolish, my editor. This book is better because she encouraged me to be even more practical than I thought I had already been. Her input, as always, is greatly appreciated.

CONTENTS

introduction

We all *love* color. Playing with color is the happiest part of quilting. Even when the actual sewing might get tedious, color keeps us coming back for more.

The question is, if we love color, why do so many quilters say that color is scary?

I believe that what makes color scary to quilters is that it forces them to make a lasting decision.

You make color decisions all day long: What am I going to wear today? Which shoes go with this outfit? These choices, and many more each day, are made without much thought. More important, these choices are not permanent.

It feels harder to choose colors for a quilt because the color choices you make, once sewn, are final. You could make the quilt again, but who does that? Not me. No wonder you might feel a little scared by color.

Knowing why color scares you is half the battle. What comes next is figuring out how to move forward. This book is designed to help you do just that. It is a *practical* guide to color, with information that will benefit both beginning and experienced quilters alike. You will find many ideas in these pages that will make picking fabrics and colors for your quilts a happy experience.

——— THE BEST PART ———

It might make you gasp, but I don't make quilts to *have* quilts. My quilts are a lovely by-product of how I like to spend my time.

I love the challenge of designing new quilts. I revel in the vast combinations of color and pattern that are possible. I love the speediness of piecing during the daytime and the more meditative process of hand appliqué, which adds calm to my evenings. And even though writing instructions for a new book is not my favorite part of the process, I also embrace this challenge.

For me, the best part of every quilt is the time I spend picking out the colors. It can be frustrating and time consuming, but no matter how long it takes, this is my favorite part of making a quilt. Nothing replaces the satisfaction I get from seeing the result of my efforts on the design wall.

I hope that the time you spend selecting colors becomes your favorite part of quiltmaking too.

SPECIAL NOTE Because this is a book about color, it does not include in-depth piecing or appliqué instructions (otherwise I would have had to cut back on the color information). If you have a preferred method for piecing or appliqué, please feel free to use it. If you are a beginner, I suggest you refer to *The Best-Ever Appliqué Sampler* by Linda Jenkins and me (from C&T Publishing), or any of our other appliqué books, for detailed appliqué instructions. For piecing, many good books are available, ranging from *Start Quilting with Alex Anderson* to *The Practical Guide to Patchwork* by Elizabeth Hartman (both from C&T Publishing), as well as many online resources.

Page 4 photos by
Becky Goldsmith: A, B, D–K • Celia Goldsmith: C

the color wheel

Color wheels are pretty, and that's why we like looking at them. Beyond being pretty, however, a color wheel is a powerful tool that shows the relationships between colors. This is important because knowing how colors work together will help you use color better in your quilts.

Some people have spent their lives studying color theory. I am not one of them. I do have a degree in interior design, and what I learned in school has been valuable—but you do not need a college degree to be able to use a color wheel. I promise.

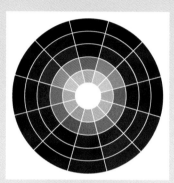

The color wheel

FOR MORE INFORMATION _____

Remember that this book is a *practical* guide to color. If you are interested, you can study more (much, much more) about color theory than I will tell you in this book. Where to start? Search the Internet for "color theory" and start clicking. Read books; a lot of them have been written on color. Refer also to Online Color Resources (page 111) for some of my favorite websites about color.

HOW THE COLOR WHEEL WORKS

It is easier to use a color wheel if you know why it is put together the way it is. The color wheels in this book are divided into twelve wedges that represent the twelve basic colors. There are more complex color wheels, with more colors and wedges, but for this book, a simple color wheel works best.

Besides being divided into wedges, the color wheel is also divided into five concentric rings. The colors are lighter in the rings toward the center and darker in the rings to the outside.

The True Colors

The middle ring on the color wheel is occupied by the *truest color*, or hue, in each wedge.

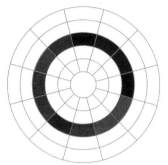

The truest colors occupy the middle ring.

Primary Colors

Primary colors are the only colors on the wheel that are not made from combining other colors. They are positioned an equal distance apart, separating the wheel into thirds.

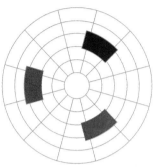

Primary colors cannot be made from other colors.

Secondary Colors

Secondary colors are halfway between the primary colors and are made by mixing together the two nearest primary colors.

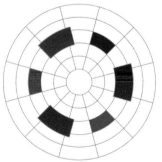

Secondary colors fall halfway between the primary colors.

Tertiary Colors

Tertiary means "third in order or level," and that is an apt description of these colors. *Tertiary colors* fall between adjacent primary and secondary colors and are a mix of the colors on either side.

Now that you know how it works, the color wheel is pretty easy to decipher.

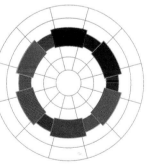

Tertiary colors fall between adjacent primary and secondary colors.

NEUTRALS

Neutral colors (white, gray, black, beige, brown) rarely show up on the color wheel. They are not associated with any specific color, although some neutrals do have undertones of one color or another.

Even though they are not "colorful," neutrals are very important to quilters. Colors shine against them, which is why you so often see neutrals used as backgrounds. Solid neutrals, in particular, showcase the colors and fabrics that they are paired with. Refer to *Tile Tango* (page 79) and *Pick-Up Sticks* (page 89).

When neutrals are used by themselves, the resulting quilts can be calm—or exciting. *Put a Bird on It* (page 64) is an example of a calm combination of neutrals. *Say Something* (page 84), made from a variety of black-and-white fabrics only, is a quilt that is anything but calm.

Neutrals are not associated with any specific color.

About Black-and-White Prints

When you buy black-and-white prints, it is because you want both black and white. However, you need to be aware that these prints can look gray in your quilt.

A black-and-white print with more white space is more likely to read as distinctly black and white. Prints that have small or thin black motifs set closely together, without much white space, can appear to be gray when viewed from a distance.

If you want your quilt to read truly black and white, use prints that have more open areas of white between the areas of black.

Black-and-white prints

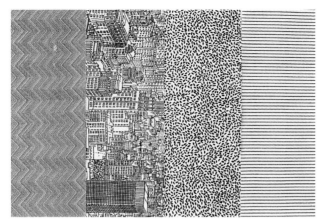

From afar, prints that have small black motifs set closely together can appear gray.

I can't always see which fabrics will appear to be gray with my eyes. When I am making a black-and-white quilt, I photograph the fabrics in the stack before cutting to test for "grayness." I don't always take out the gray fabrics, but I am careful with them. I photograph the quilt in progress as well.

COLOR TEMPERATURE

Warm colors range from yellow to red-violet. They have a reputation for being comfy, cozy, embracing colors.

Cool colors range from yellow-green to blue-violet. They might be considered calm, sophisticated, and less emotional.

You may have read that warm colors come forward in a composition and that cool colors recede. Sometimes that is true, and sometimes it isn't. To my eye, what determines a color's place on the visual plane depends on clarity, value, and the other colors in view, as you will see as you read on.

Because this is a practical guide to color, rather than a treatise on color theory, I can say that I rarely think about the temperature of a color. I know which colors make me happy, and those are the colors that I buy and use, regardless of their temperature.

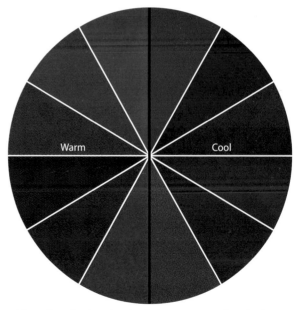

The color wheel can be divided into warm and cool colors.

color schemes

An unlimited number of color combinations exist. In fact, so many choices are possible that some quilters find it hard to know where to begin.

When in doubt, you can look to the color wheel for inspiration. You will find color combinations that are practically without fail. This is one reason understanding how the color wheel works is so valuable.

As you become more comfortable working with color, you'll find yourself putting together colors that don't fit into a tidy color scheme. This is perfectly fine; not all color schemes need to be an "official" color scheme.

THE ULTIMATE 3-IN-1 COLOR TOOL

You may find that the color wheel is most helpful when you have a problem. Perhaps you have found the perfect two fabrics for a quilt, but you need one more. If you know how the color wheel works, finding that third color is much easier.

If you are not comfortable combining colors, it's a good idea to buy a small color wheel—one that you can carry with you. Joen Wolfrom's Ultimate 3-in-1 Color Tool (by C&T Publishing) is a very good choice. Spend some time with it.

Joen's color wheel is broken down into 24 different colors. Each card in the tool shows a variety of color schemes for each of the 24 colors in the wheel. The flip side of each page shows a variety of tints, shades, and grayed tones of each color.

If you work with grayed fabrics, such as Civil War prints, the clear colors on a standard color wheel don't help you much. But with this tool, you can find the grayed versions of the colors represented on the color wheel.

COLOR RELATIVITY

Color is relative. Every color is affected by the colors next to it. *Every time you combine fabrics, you have to pay attention to how those specific fabrics work together.* Context counts.

How much you use of a color matters. Palettes can be made darker or lighter, stronger or quieter, by using more or less of any color.

Because there are an infinite number of color combinations, there is never just one correct way to select colors for a quilt. Don't let yourself be overwhelmed by that knowledge. Instead, view it as a license to play with color.

— MONOCHROMATIC COLOR SCHEMES —

A *monochromatic color scheme* combines different values of only one color. This color scheme often has a calm demeanor. Working in monochrome is one way of learning how to manage differences in value without having to worry about combining different colors.

Many of the colors on the color wheel are easy to work with in monochrome. Greens, blues, purples, yellows, oranges—from the lightest pastel tints to the darkest shades, each of these is still recognizably "that" color. The same is true for neutrals. From cream to dark brown, or from white through gray to black, the different values don't turn into some other color.

It is more difficult to build a red monochromatic color scheme. Red fabrics tend to lean toward either blue or orange. As blue-reds get lighter, they turn pink. As orange-reds get lighter, they turn light rosy orange. If you want a quilt that reads "red," pink and orange are not good choices.

When I want to work with only red, I use red-and-white prints, as I did in *Round and Round* (page 37). This makes it possible to have a variety of light, medium, and dark values that read as red.

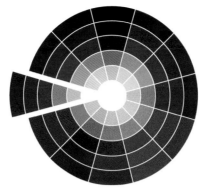

A monochromatic color scheme uses different values of only one color.

practical advice

Building a monochromatic quilt takes discipline, at least for me. I find it hard to resist the urge to add a spark of a different color. When you work in monochrome, you'll have to decide for yourself whether to stick to the plan— or not.

Be sure to choose a variety of values in your chosen color: light, medium, and dark. If you are using a pattern and it calls for a background fabric, use one from your stack if you want to stay true to the monochromatic color scheme. Refer to Value (page 17) and Building Stacks (page 45).

— COMPLEMENTARY COLOR SCHEMES —

When you combine *complementary colors*, or colors that are directly across from each other on the color wheel, the result is often dynamic and full of energy. A good example is the combination of red and green. Think of all of the times you have seen red and green together at Christmas. They always look great together.

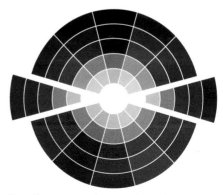

Complementary colors are those that are right across from each other on the color wheel.

You can use complementary colors in equal amounts in a composition—or use less of one color and more of the other. I used the same amounts of both blue and orange in my quilt *Opposites Attract* (page 75). White separates the two complementary colors in this quilt, giving them space to breathe.

Complementary colors orange and blue are a happy, vibrant combination in *Opposites Attract* (page 75).

practical advice

If there is one color that you want to work with but aren't sure what to pair with it, look across the color wheel to find its complement. Build stacks of fabric in these two colors (page 45). Choose light, medium, and dark values so that you have more choices as you build your quilt.

If your pattern calls for the addition of a background color, look to neutral colors or to a light (or dark) value of one of the two complementary colors.

- SPLIT COMPLEMENTARY COLOR SCHEMES -

A *split comple-mentary color scheme* is made up of one color plus the colors on either side of its complement. In this example, red is the color that determines the other two colors.

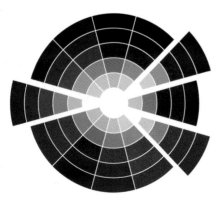

A split complementary color scheme uses one color and the colors on either side of the color's complement.

Pot of Flowers with One Blue Pot (page 20) is a nice example of a split complementary color scheme. There is more red and yellow-green in this quilt. There is not as much aqua blue, but because this blue is so different from the red and green, it is the focal point of the quilt.

I used the same, slightly expanded, split complementary color scheme in *The Ground (As Seen from Above)* (next page). The quilt is predominantly yellow-green, with a mix of reds and some purples. Aqua blue, the third color in this color scheme, is used less, but it is still an important accent color.

The Ground (As Seen from Above), 71″ × 39″, by Becky Goldsmith, 2007

Although this quilt is mostly green and red, little bits of aqua add an important spark to it.

practical advice

You don't have to stop with just three colors. For example, if one of the three colors is a true blue, you might add a blue-violet that blends into the true blue. You might be moving beyond the strict definition of a split complementary color scheme, but that's okay. The key is to pay attention to how the blues look together—and then to how all of the colors look together. Refer to Building Stacks (page 45).

TRIADIC COLOR SCHEMES

A *triadic color scheme* uses three colors that are an equal distance apart on the color wheel. If you superimposed an equilateral triangle over the color wheel, these colors would be at the points. This is a good color scheme to use when choosing the colors for a three-color quilt.

Square Play (page 70) is a quilt made with the three primary colors (red, blue, and yellow) that make up a triadic color scheme. I chose these colors intentionally as a personal challenge, because when I imagine primary colors, I see crayons and clowns, and that is not usually the look I am going for in a quilt.

What worked for me was to make red the dominant color, with vibrant accents of blue and yellow. The finished quilt looks more like a red bandana than a box of crayons.

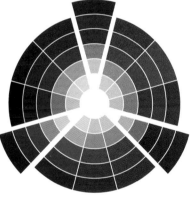

A triadic color scheme is made up of three colors that are an equal distance apart on the color wheel.

Square Play (page 70)

Red, blue, and yellow, the primary colors, are a triadic color scheme.

practical advice

You can always choose colors that are less bright, darker, or grayer to make any of the color schemes. For example, I could have combined pastel versions of red, blue, and yellow, and it would still be a triadic color scheme.

You can also choose colors that are close to the base colors. For example, I added orange-reds and blue-reds to the primary shade of red in Square Play. Be sure to pay attention to how the different shades look together. If you veer too far from your base color, it might be distracting—or it might add just the right amount of interest to the quilt. You'll know better as you begin putting the pieces together on your design wall.

QUADRATIC COLOR SCHEMES

A *quadratic color scheme* uses four colors that are an equal distance apart on a color wheel that has twelve sections. If you superimposed a square over the color wheel, these colors would be at the corners of the square.

I have never *set out* to make a quilt with a quadratic color scheme, but that doesn't mean that I haven't done it. The colors in *Thistles* came together naturally.

When you look at the four colors in any quadradic color scheme, it is helpful to remember that you do not have to use them in equal amounts. Gold is the dominant color in *Thistles*, followed by green, violet, and blue.

A quadratic color scheme is made up of four colors that are an equal distance apart on the color wheel.

practical advice

Don't let any of these color schemes become the boss of you. Remember that you are making the decisions. If you think you need more or fewer colors in your quilt, no one is going to chase you down and tell you that you can't change the plan.

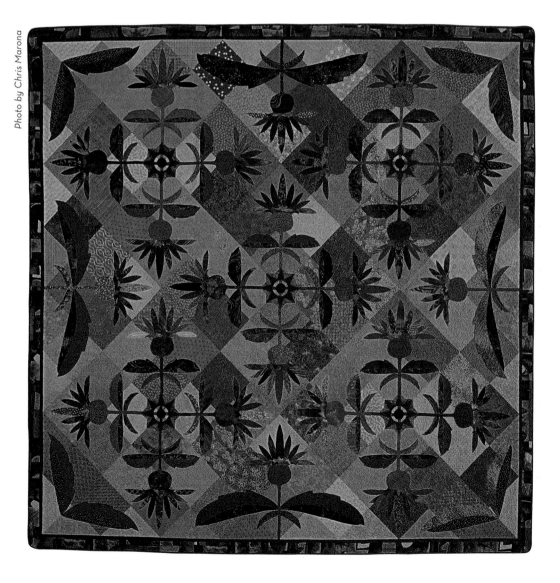

Photo by Chris Marona

Thistles, 71″ × 71″, by Becky Goldsmith, 1997

A quadratic color scheme of violet, blue, green, and orange-gold is evident in *Thistles*.

ANALOGOUS COLOR SCHEMES

Analogous colors are those that are next to each other on the color wheel. They blend together happily.

A smooth transition from one color to another adds movement to a quilt. You can see this in *Picasso's Garden*, where the blending of colors encourages you to look up and down the vines.

Even when you choose colors that blend together, you do not have to use them right next to each other in the quilt. You can spread them around and still retain that beautiful, harmonious look.

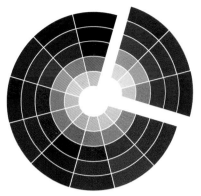

Analogous colors are next to each other on the color wheel.

practical advice

When I choose a color for a quilt, I almost always add colors that are analogous to it in my stacks of fabric. This is true no matter what sort of color scheme I am using. These "extra" colors provide subtle shading that adds depth and interest to a quilt.

Picasso's Garden, 49″ × 57″, by Becky Goldsmith, 2007

Blues that blend into both purple and green are analogous colors that shine against the neutral browns in the background.

RAINBOW COLOR SCHEMES

Rainbow color schemes are happy—your eyes are drawn to the movement and beauty of many colors blending together around the color wheel. If you are observant, you can see rainbows of color in all sorts of places.

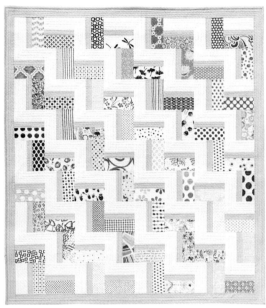

Stairway to Heaven (page 106)

Soft rainbows are lovely too.

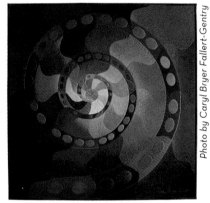

The Glory Window, designed by Gabriel Loire, from the Chapel of Thanksgiving, designed by architect Philip Johnson, located in Dallas, Texas

The Glory Window from the Chapel of Thanksgiving is an eye-catching example of colors that blend like a rainbow.

Caryl Bryer Fallert-Gentry is a master when it comes to using rainbow color schemes in quilts. Her quilt *Spirogyra #5* is a fine example. The spiral movement in the quilt design is enhanced as one color blends into another. This quilt invites the viewer in for a longer stay.

Spirogyra #5, 30" × 30", by Caryl Bryer Fallert-Gentry, 2012 • bryerpatch.com

Spirogyra #5 is a fine example of the use of a rainbow color scheme.

Rainbow fabrics do not have to be bright and bold; they can also be soft and light. Feel free to play with the intensity of the colors in your rainbow to suit the mood of your quilt. I had fun using a softer rainbow of colors in *Stairway to Heaven.*

If you look at the colorful fabric in this quilt, you might notice that the colors in the prints are not necessarily soft. For instance, the reds in the red prints are dark and bright. What makes these fabrics seem lighter and softer is that there is so much white in each of the prints.

practical advice

To build a rainbow, choose the color and value that you want to work with the most. If your choice is a print, choose one that is predominantly one color, not multicolored. Follow the colors on the color wheel and build a stack of fabric, blending from one color into the next color until you have worked all the way around the wheel. Refer to Building Stacks (page 45).

Another strategy is to begin with a stack of solids or prints that are already arranged in a rainbow. You can sometimes find fat quarter rainbow packs in a quilt shop. Add more fabric to fill out your rainbow.

value and contrast

What could be more important than color? Color is the exciting, *look-at-me-NOW* attention getter. However, as fantastic as color is, the contrast between colors and values is the most important thing in the design of your quilts.

The word *contrast* has many definitions, but I find this one from dictionary.com to be the most meaningful to quilters: Contrast is an *"opposition ... of different forms, lines, or colors in a work of art to intensify each element's properties and produce a more dynamic expressiveness."*

What does that even mean? Simply stated, it means that there are many kinds of contrast: contrast between values, colors, scales, and textures. You need to understand each of these kinds of contrast because you will use them all.

Contrast between the elements in your design makes different areas of your quilt more (or less) visible. Contrast marks the difference between one shape and another, between *foreground* and *background* (see The Structure of a Quilt, page 39).

───── VALUE ─────

Every color has a *value*. It will be light, medium, dark—or somewhere in between.

Value refers to how light or dark a color is. The two smaller, inside rings in the color wheel are lighter—white has been added to the basic hue. These lighter colors are called *tints*.

The two large outer rings in the color wheel are darker. Black has been added to the basic hue. These darker colors are called *shades*.

Value refers to how light or dark a color is.

When light and dark values are placed next to each other, they are easy to tell apart. The line that is formed between them is very visible. This is *high contrast*.

When the contrast is high, it is easy to see the difference between the light and dark values.

When values that are similar to each other are placed together, they are harder to tell apart. The line between them blurs. This is *low* contrast.

When the contrast is low, it is harder to see differences between the similar values.

High contrast is neither better nor worse than low contrast. How you manipulate the areas that are high and low in contrast is the important thing. As you look at quilts in this book and elsewhere, pay attention to how value is used to reinforce the design of the quilt as a whole.

Some quilts rely on strong contrast. The words *tiny* and *huge* are the first things you see when you look at *Say Something* (page 84). That was my intention. Now imagine if the words were made from one of the light prints used in the background. The words would disappear, dissipating the impact of the quilt.

In some quilts, low contrast is called for. *Stairway to Heaven* (page 106) is a quiet quilt with elements that are low in contrast with each other. However, even though none of the fabrics is particularly dark, there is enough contrast between the white, gray, and colored prints to be able to differentiate one part of the quilt from another.

Look at *Indian Orange Peel* by Karen K. Stone. In some of the units, Karen combined two fabrics that contrast each other. In these areas the design is most visible. In other areas, she sewed together fabrics that are very similar in value. The pattern almost disappears in these areas.

The high-contrast units are sharp and in focus. The low-contrast units are softer and out of focus. The combination of high- and low-value contrast, along with the use of clear and gray colors, gives Karen's quilt movement and depth, making it a quilt that is very interesting to spend time with.

LOW VOLUME

A *loud* quilt would be one with strong colors and contrasts. A *low-volume* quilt is the opposite of that—one where the noise has been turned down. Low-volume quilts are made solely with fabrics considered *light* in value.

When you combine light fabrics, some will be darker than others. The contrast is still there, but it is less strong than it would be if much-darker fabrics were added to the mix.

I actually prefer to call these light quilts *quiet*, rather than low-volume, because I find *quiet* to be more visually descriptive. But no matter what you call them, quiet quilts have an attitude all their own.

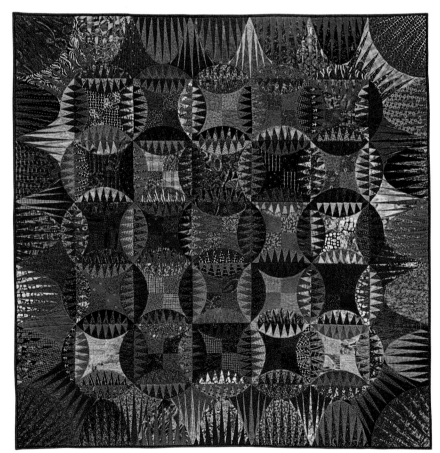

Indian Orange Peel, 63″ × 63″, by Karen K. Stone, 1994 • karenkstone.com

The high-contrast units in *Indian Orange Peel* are sharp, in focus. The low-contrast units are softer, out of focus.

COLOR AND CONTRAST

When quilters talk about *contrast*, they are usually talking about the contrast between values: light versus dark. But contrast is not about value alone. Colors contrast as well. Simply stated, we can see differences between colors, even when the values are similar.

Colors that are farther apart on the color wheel are more obviously different from each other. This is especially true for complementary colors (page 11). Even when the colors are similar in value, it is usually not hard to tell one complementary color from another.

It is easy to see the difference between red and green, complementary colors, even though the values are similar.

It is harder to see the difference between colors that are similar in value and that lie close together on the color wheel, like analogous colors (page 15).

It is harder to see the difference between red and orange, analogous colors that are similar in value.

What this means in practice is that even though different colors are very similar in value, sometimes colors still have enough contrast between them for us to be able to easily tell them apart. For example, the complementary colors of red and green in *Lorna's Vine* are similar in value but still easy to tell apart.

Lorna's Vine, 71″ × 71″, by Becky Goldsmith, 2006

In this quilt, the complementary colors red and green are similar in value but still easy to tell apart.

But this is not always the case. Sometimes colors that are different from each other blend together, making it harder to tell them apart. The orangey reds in the wheels in the setting blocks blend into the gold backgrounds behind them because they are similar in value *and* they are close together on the color wheel.

The blues in the wheel blocks are both darker in value and a very different color from the other colors used in the quilt. The blues stand out and make the setting blocks interesting.

I chose these colors and values for the wheels because I wanted half of the spokes to stand out. They look like fringed flowers to me.

WHAT DO YOU SEE?

We are programmed to notice what is different. When we let our eyes wander, they tend to settle on the most different thing in our field of vision.

Pot of Flowers with One Blue Pot is a perfect example of how something different in a quilt can grab and hold your attention.

I was impressed that a quilter from the 1860s was so bold. Imagine the nerve it must have taken to use blue in what would otherwise have been a traditional red and green quilt. Then I found out that the one blue pot was an accident. It is the result of an unstable overdyed green fabric in which the yellow dye has migrated to the back of the quilt. But that blue block is what makes this quilt special.

After seeing this quilt years ago, I became much more willing to let go of the "rules." I embrace asymmetry and quirkiness in my own quilts, and I celebrate when I see them in other people's quilts, as I did when I first saw Latifah Saafir's quilt *Convergence.*

Pot of Flowers with One Blue Pot, 86" × 86". The maker and provenance are unknown, c 1860. From the collection of Debra Grana. This quilt was acquired in an upstate New York auction.

When you look at this quilt, what do you see?

practical advice

Try it. Look around and without thinking about it, pay attention to what catches your eye. It might be dark or light, big or small, but whatever it is, your eyes will be drawn to the thing that contrasts the most with what is around it.

Photo by Becky Goldsmith

What catches your eye?

The pattern in *Convergence* is powerful. There is a subtle tension between the focal points—my eyes follow the curved lines to the points where they converge, but they are also drawn to the two blue lines. It would be a lovely quilt if all of the lines were red, but it is that bit of blue that makes this quilt special.

The splash of unexpected color makes both of these quilts memorable and a little bit quirky. The opposite of "memorable and quirky" is "forgettable and boring"—no one wants to make quilts that fall into that category.

Convergence, 61″ × 73″, by Latifah Saafir, 2012 • thequiltengineer.com
This quilt employs a similar spark of color that makes it memorable.

BE BRAVE

Dare to be at least a little bit quirky. You don't have to have one wildly different thing in every quilt, but you can move beyond the expected.

For example, if you are making a scrap quilt that is mostly blue and green, add a little bit of something that is different enough to be noticed. You could add a few colors that are related to your first colors, like purple or yellow-green, and your quilt will have more personality.

Flip through the book and you will notice that my quilts rarely have a single, very strong focal point. Instead, I rely on an interesting mix of colors, values, and visual textures to make the quilt as a whole engaging. I often choose fabrics that are not typical or obvious choices.

Tick Tock (page 98) is a good example of this. The fabrics in the background are active, not quiet. The background does not disappear, but neither does it overpower the appliqué. The quilt as a whole demands that you spend time looking at it.

If you would like to try being quirky but are not sure where to start, try this: Start making a quilt, but about halfway through, choose a few fabrics and pretend that you have run out of them. Look in your stash for fabric that is similar in color or value—but not too similar—and finish the quilt with the substitute fabric.

the nature of fabric

Quilters paint with fabric. Just as you would expect a painter to understand how paint works, a quilter needs to understand how fabric works.

Fabric falls into two broad categories: predictable and unpredictable. Predictable fabrics are not better or worse than unpredictable fabrics—they just behave differently.

Most of the fabric that quilters use falls into the predictable category. A **predictable fabric** is one that is not a surprise when you cut it up. If you are making a quilt cut from strips, a predictable fabric is your friend. When you cut a predictable fabric into smaller squares, the print looks basically the same everywhere you place it.

An **unpredictable fabric** is likely to offer surprises when it is cut into small pieces. Unpredictable fabrics are most often large-scale prints or multicolored fabrics with large repeats. These fabrics don't work as well in quilts made from strips of fabric because it is hard to know what color will dominate any particular small piece that is cut from the larger print.

━━━━ PREDICTABLE FABRICS ━━━━

Solids

Solid-color fabric is the most predictable kind. No matter how you cut it, the color remains the same in every piece.

Solids are very versatile. They can be used with other solids or combined with prints. Depending on how you use them, solids can be quiet and unobtrusive (imagine a white background), or they can take center stage.

Solid fabric is very versatile and can be used with other solids or with prints.

It's easy to think of solids as boring, but quilts made with only solid fabrics are wonderfully graphic, whether the quilt is traditional or modern in design.

Amish Baskets, 49″ × 49″, by Linda Jenkins, 2006

Quilts made with only solid fabrics are wonderfully graphic and fresh.

Textured Solids

The Postimpressionist painter Van Gogh used textured brushstrokes to give his paintings energy. You can use textured solids in a similar way to add movement to the quieter areas of your quilt.

Textured solids look solid from a distance, and they too are very predictable. Only as you get closer do you see the details in the print. Tone-on-tone prints are the most common kind of textured solid, combining more than one value of the same color.

Tone-on-tone prints are active solids.

Single-color, mottled hand-dyes and batiks are another kind of textured solid. They have a fluid visual texture without a distinctive pattern. When you want more than a flat, solid color in your quilt, add some textured solids into the mix.

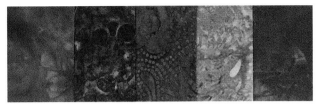

Single-color mottled hand-dyes and batiks have a more fluid visual texture.

Art quilters often create amazing quilts by using solids and textured solids much as they would paint. Laura Wasilowski is an expert at this. In her quilt *Five Sisters*, Laura goes beyond a simple use of solids to create a variety of interesting details. The five orange leaves are not cut from a printed fabric. Laura cut and fused strips and dots to an orange base fabric to create those lovely, complex leafy sisters.

Photo by Laura Wasilowski

Five Sisters, 51" × 51", by Laura Wasilowski, 2006 • artfabrik.com

Five Sisters is a marvelous example of the expressiveness of solid fabrics.

practical advice:

Textured solids never go out of style, so it's a good idea to maintain a nice supply of them in your stash. You don't need yards of any one fabric. Instead, collect a wide variety of fat quarters so that you have lots of colors and values to choose from when you want them.

Predictable Prints

All printed fabric has contrast between the colors and values *inside the print itself*. The contrast found in the print relates directly to how quiet or active the fabric appears to be.

Printed fabrics have repeating patterns across the width and length of the fabric. The *repeat* refers to the length of the pattern before it repeats itself again. The repetition of shapes and colors gives the print a cohesive appearance. The smaller the pattern and repeat, the easier it is to predict what the fabric will look like when it is cut up.

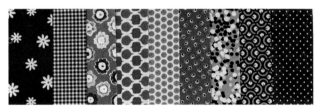

Small, regular prints are predictable.

When you make a pieced quilt, you rarely cut all your individual pieces of fabric to audition together on your design wall. You are more likely to construct units or blocks that you then look at. A predictable print can be cut into big or small pieces and will look the same everywhere it shows up in the quilt. In pieced quilts, that is a very good thing.

LOOKING THROUGH WINDOWS

Looking at fabric through a window template helps you see what that fabric will look like when it is cut into pieces. To make a window template, cut a square of heavy white paper or poster board with a "window" opening in the center. The opening can be any size you like. Leave at least 2″ of paper on each side of the window opening.

Place the window template on the right side of the fabric and see how the print looks. Move the template around on the fabric. If the fabric is predictable, it will look just about the same no matter where you place the window.

When you go to the quilt shop, carry window templates in a variety of sizes with you. Use them on fabric that you might not normally buy. You may be surprised at what you see.

Use a window template to help you visualize what a print will look like when it is cut.

DOTS

You don't have to see much of a dotted fabric to know what it is and what it would look like if you could see more of it. That is the essence of predictability.

The smooth edges and the regular shape of dots lend them a calm, yet perky, attitude. In my humble opinion, dots can be used with just about any other fabric.

Dots mix well with every other fabric.

CIRCULAR DESIGNS

Many predictable prints have circular designs that may not technically be dots but behave in much the same way. A circular design has more visual texture (page 36) than a traditional, smooth dot, which is what makes circular designs interesting in a composition.

As with other predictable prints, these prints will retain their look whether you cut 2″ × 2″ or 6″ × 6″ squares.

Dotlike prints behave much like smooth dots when cut into small pieces.

FLOWERS AND ZIGZAGS AND PENGUINS—OH MY!

An unlimited number of motifs can be printed on fabric, and any of them can be predictable. However, you may be avoiding some fabrics because, for whatever reason, they feel less safe to you.

Quilters often avoid prints such as these that feel less safe.

I love, love, love interesting and unusual prints! They add a special spark to my quilts. Yes, you have to pick and choose where to use them, but unless you don't use printed fabric at all, you absolutely want to have these kinds of prints in your palette of fabrics.

If a print catches your eye, don't pass it by—even if it is something outside of your comfort zone. Use a window template to see what that fabric will look like when cut into pieces. You may be surprised.

Look again. When cut smaller, these prints still look like the fabric they came from.

IDENTIFYING PREDICTABLE

How can you tell at a glance if a print is predictable? I look at the density of the printed motifs on the fabric. Are they close together, or are they widely scattered? The closer the motifs are, the more likely it is that small pieces will look like the fabric they were cut from.

I also look at the distribution of colors across the face of the fabric. I ask myself: If I cut this up, will I see the same mix of colors in the smaller pieces?

It may not be easy at first, but identifying predictable prints does get easier with practice and is a good skill to have.

Conversation Prints

Conversation prints (sometimes called novelty prints) have identifiable "things" on them: bugs, teddy bears, Mount Rushmore. ... Whatever the thing is, it is intended to be seen. Viewers notice these things—they might even have a conversation about them.

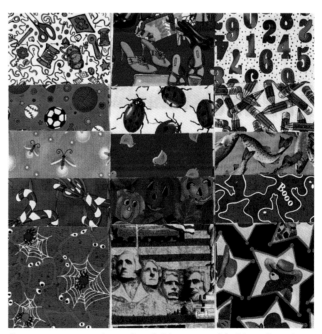

Conversation prints have identifiable, very visible "things" on them.

Conversation prints are perfect for children's quilts, where the intention is for the child to pick out different things in the fabric. These prints can be fun to use in seasonal quilts or in quilts with a theme.

I use conversation prints sparingly because I don't necessarily want the viewer to pick out a bug in the fabric before they see the design of the quilt itself. But these prints are fun to have in your stash.

Directional Fabric

Directional fabrics have lines in the design and are, in general, very predictable. Stripes and plaids are the most obvious kinds of directional fabric.

Lines—whether they are long or short, smooth or rough—add movement to a composition. Lines point us in one direction or another, and our eyes glide along them, stopping where the lines stop. You can cut the fabric lengthwise to get one look or crosswise for a different look.

PRINTED STRIPES

Stripes can be printed on fabric or woven into the cloth. There are all kinds of printed stripes: simple and smooth, multicolored, stripes with the same or varying widths—the possibilities are endless.

Printed stripes are available in a huge variety of sizes and colors.

Stripes can be made from a variety of motifs that are stacked into lines to create a more complex striped pattern. Our eyes can detect the lines in the overall pattern, and those lines still imply movement.

practical advice: *Conversation prints can be predictable in the same way that other prints can be predictable. When you cut them up, the smaller pieces of the fabric reflect the look of the fabric as a whole.*

I have placed conversation prints in their own category because the motifs in the fabric call attention to themselves in a different way from the motifs in most other prints. They don't blend into the larger pattern of the quilt; instead they demand to be noticed. If that is what you want, conversation prints can be fun to use.

practical advice: *When working with directional fabrics, I do not usually spend time making sure that I am cutting exactly with the grain, on the lines in the fabric. Roberta Horton taught me—and thousands of other quilters—that cutting "casually off-grain" is both lovely and less stressful.*

That said, there are times when it is important to cut directional fabric exactly. When the pattern calls for it, I do take the time to do just that.

Motifs can be stacked in rows to create a more complex striped pattern.

WOVEN STRIPES

Woven stripes are formed when the lengthwise threads in the fabric are dyed different colors and are woven together. Woven stripes are predictable in the same way that printed stripes are. However, colorwise, woven stripes are a little different.

Woven stripes are formed when different colors of thread are woven together.

When the different colors of thread are woven together, they blend to make new colors. The new colors are closely related to the colors that they have been woven from. These more nuanced colors make woven stripes a good choice when you need a fabric to transition from one color to another.

For example, if you are making a quilt from blues and reds and you need a fabric to bridge the color gap between them, a stripe woven from similar blue and red threads will form purple bridge colors.

PLAIDS

Plaids are made from crossed lines.

Your eyes glide down a long stripe, but your eyes stay put when you look at a plaid because the lines are interrupted. In that sense, a plaid is static, much like any other nondirectional printed fabric. However, the lines in plaids offer a nice counterpoint to curvier prints.

Unfortunately, plaid fabrics are not easy to find. When you find one you like, you should definitely add it to your stash.

Woven Plaids

Woven plaids are formed when different colors of thread are woven across each other to make a pattern. The resulting plaid pattern can be small or large, single colored or multicolored.

Woven plaids are always on the straight of grain. Like woven stripes, the colors blend to make new colors. The lines and colors formed are softer and more nuanced than they are in printed plaids. Plaids, too, make excellent blender fabrics.

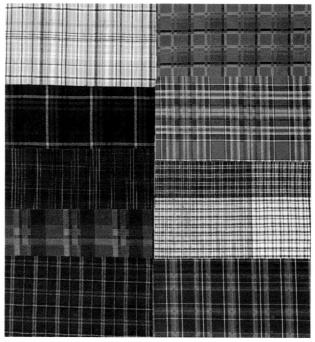

Woven plaids are always on the straight of grain.

Printed Plaids

Printed plaids mimic woven plaids but are not limited by the direction of the threads in the cloth. In fact, the lines in a printed plaid do not have to be "lines" at all. They can be dots or slashes or flowers—the options are limitless.

The lines in a printed plaid do not have to be "lines"—and they can be printed on the bias grain of the fabric.

UNPREDICTABLE FABRICS

Unpredictable fabrics are often large-scale prints or multicolored fabrics with large repeats. Because the designs in the fabric are big or the colors widely dispersed, it's hard to know what you are going to get when you cut the fabric into smaller pieces.

If you are making a quilt cut from strips, you can't predict which color will end up where, and this can play havoc in repeating blocks. That said, once you understand them, unpredictable prints do have a role to play in quilting.

NOTE Remember that you can use a window template to help you evaluate whether or not a particular big print has a predictable pattern. Refer to Looking through Windows (page 24).

Big Prints

Big prints have an expansive feeling that is directly related to their large size. The motifs appear oversized next to other quilt fabric. The colors in these prints are often bold and bright and spaced widely apart. This print, Vivienne from Alexander Henry Fabrics, is a good example.

In appliqué, you can fussy cut shapes from different parts of the print. In piecing, you can fussy cut a fabric, but generally you begin by cutting strips. Strips and other small shapes cut from a large-print fabric are different enough that they could have come from four different fabrics. In a quilt pattern that requires regular color placement, that can be either a problem—or a virtue.

It's hard to tell that these squares came from the same piece of fabric.

The colors in a big print look good together; they don't clash. Different colors may dominate the various shapes cut from a big print, but these shapes will be color coordinated. If you set them against a common background, the results can be exciting.

Needle in a Haystack is a fun, two-fabric quilt. I would have had to work a lot harder to get the same effect from individual red, blue, and yellow fabrics.

Big prints can be wild, with big designs and colors widely dispersed.

Needle in a Haystack, 36″ × 36″, by Becky Goldsmith, 2014
Strips cut from the big print shine against a white background.

TRY THEM— YOU'LL LIKE THEM___

Big prints feel open and expansive, even when they are cut into small pieces. They add a particular kind of movement to a quilt. The scale of a big print especially stands out when combined with smaller-scale prints or solids. I would encourage you to keep some in your stash. It will be even better if you remember to use them.

Easier-to-Use Big Prints

Some big prints are more predictable than others. Look for big prints where the colors are mixed together well across the face of the print. This fabric, designed by Philip Jacobs for Rowan Westminster Fabrics, is a good example.

You can cut a variety of shapes from this fabric. Each shape will retain the look of the fabric it was cut from, and that look will be distinctly different from smaller, tighter, more predictable prints.

These smaller squares are obviously cut from the same big print.

Big prints with colors that are mixed together well across the face of the print are more predictable.

Big-Print Quilt Backs

Another way to use big prints is to put them on the back of a quilt. Big prints make great quilt backs, especially if you want to hide the quilting stitches on the back of your quilt.

I often sew different big prints together, in no particular pattern, until I have constructed a quilt back of the correct size.

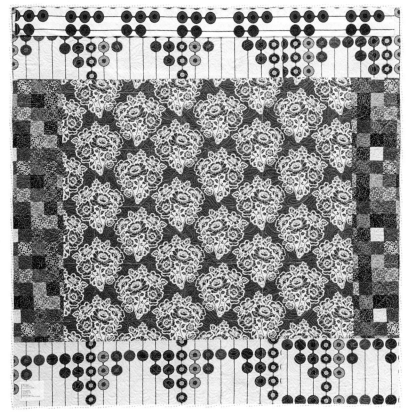

The back of *Tile Tango* (page 79) is made from a combination of big prints.

Unpredictable Hand-Dyes

Hand-dyed fabric that has widely spaced areas of dense color falls into the "unpredictable" category.

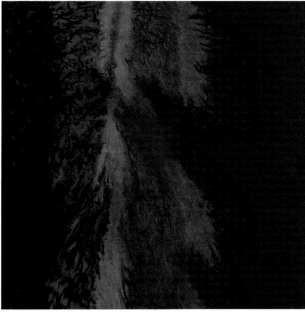

Multicolored hand-dyes can have bold areas of color that are widely dispersed.

Small squares cut from this fabric have nothing in common among them. They look as if they came from several different fabrics. That's great if you are fussy cutting, but this kind of fabric can be harder to use in rotary-cut piecing projects.

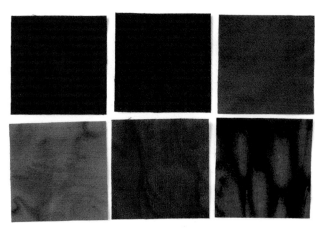

These 2½" squares cut from a multicolored hand-dyed fabric look as if they came from several different fabrics.

clarity

Clarity means clearness. Clean water, fresh air—these are physical embodiments of clarity.

Clear colors are pure and clean. The opposite of clear colors would be colors that are muddy or gray.

—— DISTANCE AND COLOR ——

When you are outside and look into the distance, you will notice that things get grayer as they get farther away. Sometimes objects are darker or lighter or bluer, but colors are always less clear. In the photo below, you can see the crisp, clear greens in the plants close to you. The same plants are less and less clearly green on the cliffs in the distance.

Gray, muted colors tend to sit back quietly, giving a quilt a more subdued attitude. When quilts are made exclusively with grayed colors, the combination of values creates the depth of field.

Photo by Becky Goldsmith

In nature, colors in the distance lose clarity and become grayer.

Your brain knows that colors fade in the distance. This is one way that you discern distance, and you do it without being aware of it. You just know that those things are farther away.

It makes sense that when you look at clear and gray colors together in quilts, your brain applies a similar kind of distance perception.

Jacob's Ladder, 66" × 75", by Becky Goldsmith, 2009

The use of grayed colors in *Jacob's Ladder* gives this quilt a more laid-back attitude.

Quilts made with only clear colors are generally more active, happy, and "in your face." When compared to quilts made with grayer colors, clear-color quilts spring forward. You can see this in *Dolly Madison's Star*, where all of the colors are up front—almost in your face.

Dolly Madison's Star, by Becky Goldsmith, 75″ × 75″, 2004. Reprinted with permission from American Patchwork and Quilting, ©2005, Meredith Corporation. All rights reserved. Subject to national and international intellectual property laws and treaties.

The clean and clear polka dot fabrics in *Dolly Madison's Star* spring toward you.

— COMBINING CLEAR AND GRAY COLORS —

Combining clear and gray colors can enhance the sense of depth and dimension in a quilt. Gray colors fall back, away from you; clear colors come forward. You can use this knowledge to manipulate the illusion of depth in your quilts. For example, the clear blues in *Box of Rain* (page 94) jump out, while the quieter gray-blues sit well back.

After you become aware of this phenomenon, you will see it in every quilt that you look at. Take a moment and flip through this book (or any other quilt book for that matter). Look at each quilt. Notice the colors that come forward; then pay attention to the colors that you don't notice so much. I would bet that you find the clearer colors coming forward and the grayer colors pushing back.

It is often easier to see this effect in quilts that you did not make. In your own quilts, you know why you made the fabric choices that you did. It can be hard to tell whether your choices have the intended effect because it is so easy to see what you expect to see. In that case, take a photo of your quilt and look at it, not the quilt.

Box of Rain (page 94)

The clearer colors in *Box of Rain* pop, while the grayer colors sit back.

practical advice

Many of us have both clear and gray colors in our stash. Sometimes they work well together, but at other times they look so bad when placed next to each other that they make your teeth hurt.

The key to using clear and gray colors comes from under-standing how they work together. In general, gray colors recede, and clear colors come forward.

COLOR CLARITY AND FABRIC

Every color is affected by what it is next to. A piece of fabric may look bright and clear next to one fabric and muddy and dull next to another fabric.

Between very clear and very gray colors is an infinite range of colors that look either clear or gray, depending on what they are next to.

In many cases, very gray colors clash when placed next to very clear colors.

Very gray colors next to very clear colors can clash.

Some fabrics can be used to bridge the gap from one end of the clarity spectrum to the other. I often turn to multicolored prints or woven plaids and stripes when I am looking for transition fabrics.

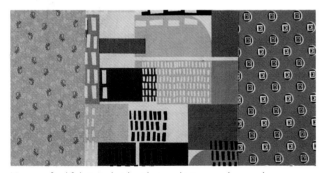

You can find fabric to bridge the gap between clear and gray colors.

If you are working with very vibrant colors, you might find a need to quiet them down. Colors that are somewhat gray can soften the impact of very clear colors. This is helpful when you want to tone down bright colors.

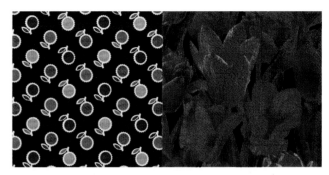

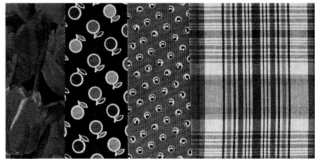

Add colors that are less clear if you want to tone down very vibrant colors.

Conversely, clearer colors can add light and dimension to a gray color palette.

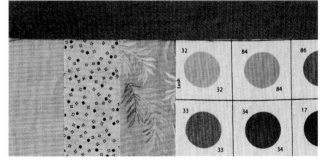

Clear colors can add light and dimension to a gray color palette.

When you are making a quilt with both gray and clear colors, remember to put the grayer colors in the background (refer to The Structure of a Quilt, page 39). The clear colors in the foreground will indeed come forward.

texture and scale

ACTUAL TEXTURE

Every fabric has an *actual texture*. Cotton, silk, denim, velvet, corduroy—each fabric has a different feel in your hand. You can almost feel the different textures as you read their names.

Every fabric has an actual texture.

Alice Beasley's quilt *All My Roads Lead to You* contains a variety of fabrics with textures that enhance the images in the quilt. The result is a quilt with rich details that is both expressive and moving.

Using textured fabric can make even a simple pieced quilt more interesting. Smooth satin catches the light, crisp silks shimmer, and soft velvet adds rich depth to a quilt. Whether you can touch them or not, you know how those textures would feel in your hand, and that stimulates a response. These kinds of fabrics may not be practical for everyday use, but they sure are pretty.

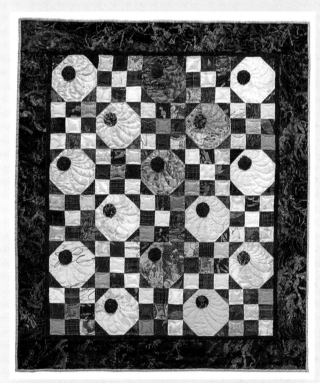

Velvet VaVoom, 38" × 44", by Becky Goldsmith, quilted by Angela Walters, 2014

Textured fabric can liven up even a simple pieced quilt.

Photo by Sibila Savage

All My Roads Lead to You, 37" × 39½", by Alice Beasley, 2011 • alicebeasley.com

Different, touchable textures, including cotton, silk, and polyester, add depth to this marvelous quilt.

ADDED TEXTURE

The cotton that quilters use has a flat surface, but it does not have to remain flat. Cotton and other fabrics can be manipulated into ripples, tucks, gathers, and more. The yo-yos in the snowball blocks in *Velvet VaVoom* (page 35) add a three-dimensional spark to the quilt surface.

A velvet yo-yo from *Velvet VaVoom* (page 35)

VISUAL TEXTURE

Cotton cloth typically used in quilting is physically smooth and flat—but it is not boring. Cotton is exciting because it is available in a huge variety of *visual textures*.

Visual texture is closely related to the scale of a print and to the contrast between the colors and values *inside the print itself*. Refer to Value and Contrast (page 17).

From solids to textured solids, from small prints to large prints, every cotton fabric has a *perceived* texture. We translate the pattern we see printed on the fabric into what it might feel like if it had actual depth. We visualize the texture—we don't actually feel it. When we look at fabric, we subconsciously ascribe a visual texture to the pattern we see.

Some fabric is printed specifically to mimic an actual texture. For example, a print might look like sky, water, wood, or stone. We know that fabric that looks like stone is not going to feel like stone, but we relate to it as if it *might*.

The visual texture of your fabric is especially important if you are making representational quilts. This would include landscapes, portraits, still lifes,

and the like—you use your fabric the way a painter uses paint to depict the subject of your quilt.

David M. Taylor's quilt *Cock of the Walk* is an excellent example of how different prints can be skillfully combined to create a new visual texture. We know that this quilt would feel like cloth, but we react to the visual textures in the fabric as if they were wood—and feathers.

Photo by David M. Taylor

Cock of the Walk, 59" × 39", by David M. Taylor, 2012 • davidtaylorquilts.com

David very skillfully used fabrics to imply the visual texture of aged wood in the background behind the rooster.

Scale refers to the size of the design in a print. Little prints look different from big prints. This is not news. In fact, it is so obvious that you may not consciously think about the scale of a print when you are combining fabrics for a quilt.

Prints can be broadly categorized as being small, medium, or large in scale.

When quilters talk about scale, they often talk about small, medium, and large prints. These are useful, but very broad, categories. In actuality, prints blend from small scale to large scale in a continuous stream.

In general, little prints are tighter, with a rougher visual texture. This is because there is often less open space around the motifs. Big prints are more expansive. Medium-scale prints fall somewhere in between.

Combining Different Scales of Prints

When you put different scales of prints together, context matters. The perceived scale of a print depends on the context in which it is used. In the photo below, the print on the right looks small when it is paired with a larger print. But if you pair the same print with an even smaller print, it no longer looks like a small print.

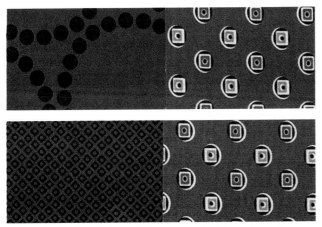

A print that looks small in one context can look large in another.

You can make a quilt using fabrics that are all similar in scale. Look closely at the prints in *The Ugly Fabric Challenge* (page 60). The scale of the individual prints is not an issue because they are nearly the same; they blend together. In many ways the sameness of the scales simplifies the quilt, focusing your attention on the play of colors in the quilt rather than on different visual textures.

In contrast, the difference between the scale of the prints in *Round and Round* makes it interesting. If this quilt were made entirely with solids or near solids, it would be lovely, with a smoother visual texture. Instead, the different sizes of high-contrast dots, stripes, and swirly prints give this quilt an assertive visual texture.

Round and Round, 48″ × 54″, by Becky Goldsmith, 2006

The different sizes of dots in *Round and Round* make this quilt interesting to look at.

Scale in Composition

Something BIG can get your attention—and so can something small. A quilt can feature something huge, or many small blocks can come together to make a pattern. Big designs are not any better than small ones—they are just different.

The rooster in David M. Taylor's quilt *Cock of the Walk* (page 36) dominates the scene. It is the perfect size for this quilt. Other equally wonderful quilts feature multiple, smaller rooster blocks. You get to decide which scale you prefer.

Compare *Cock of the Walk* with *Tile Tango*, a quilt made using 8″ × 8″ blocks that are repeated 36 times. The power of *Tile Tango* comes from the pattern formed when the blocks are set together.

Scale is important in pieced quilts as well. A quilt made from 2″ × 2″ squares is very different from a quilt made from 12″ × 12″ squares. At the very least, you can use more fabrics and colors in a quilt with lots of pieces, which explains why scrap quilts are generally made from a lot of small pieces.

Tile Tango (page 79)

The 8″ × 8″ flower blocks combine to make a very graphic statement.

the structure of a quilt

IDENTIFY THE BACKGROUND AND FOREGROUND

I have always used a simple system to build my quilts. I identify the foreground and background in every quilt I make, whether the quilt is pieced or appliquéd. A painter would refer to these as positive and negative spaces.

This is an easy concept in an appliqué quilt. The appliqué, which is the focus of the quilt, is the foreground and the positive space. The appliqué sits on top of the background, and the areas not covered by the appliqué are the negative space. The positive and negative spaces are easy to identify.

You can also identify the foreground and background in a pieced quilt, even though you may never have thought about it in quite this way. Whether a pieced quilt is simple or complex, some part of the design is more important than the rest. The dominant part of the quilt design is the foreground (positive), which may have several components. The rest is the background (negative).

practical advice

It is so easy to get caught up in the color of a quilt. You see a picture, you love the colors, and you want to make that quilt. But then something happens: Perhaps you can't find fabrics in those same colors, or the person you are making it for requests something different. It is easier to change colors if you can tease apart the background and foreground, regardless of what colors they are.

It might help to think of a pieced quilt as a puzzle. As with a puzzle, if you can see the underlying pattern, it is easier to put it together. In a quilt, when you see the background, you can see how the parts of the foreground fit together on top of it. When you see how the parts of the foreground fit together, you can more easily manipulate those parts. You can thoughtfully change colors without changing the overall pattern of the quilt.

Let's start with an easy example. In this Nine-Patch block, blue is the dominant color. It is both darker and more prevalent than the white fabric. The blue in this block is the foreground; the white is the background.

In this block, the blue is the dominant fabric. White is the background.

The same blue fabric becomes the background when it is used with a different, darker, more active fabric.

The higher the contrast between values, the more we notice the difference between them. Dark values usually demand more attention than lighter values. In both of these blocks, the dark fabric is the foreground fabric.

The solid blue from the first block is now the background fabric. The dark blue is the foreground.

Backgrounds are often the lightest value in a quilt, but that is not always the case. Backgrounds can also be dark, which pushes the lighter fabrics into the foreground. In *Amish Four-Patch*, the lighter, bright Four-Patches and the gold inner borders float on the black background.

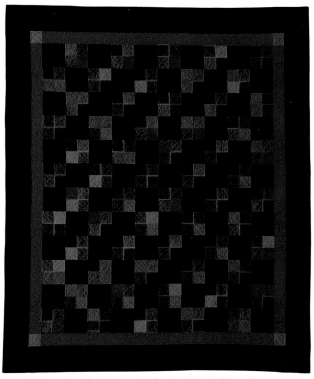

Amish Four-Patch, 52″ × 60″, by Becky Goldsmith, quilted by Mary Covey, 2007

Backgrounds are not always light. In this quilt, bright colors float on a black background.

WHY HAVE I NEVER HEARD ABOUT BACKGROUNDS LIKE THIS BEFORE?

The answer to this question is, because most traditional quiltmakers don't think this way, or if they do, they don't talk about it. It may be something that they know but don't call out.

When you read the instructions in a quilt book or pattern, you are usually instructed to buy specific amounts of fabric in the colors of the pictured quilt.

Instructions are written this way because you can refer to a photograph of the quilt. Referring to colors is a clear way to share the information so that you, the reader,

know what the writer of the pattern is talking about. Another way to share similar information is to refer to light, medium, and dark fabrics.

Although this is a good way to write yardage information, it doesn't tell you much about the structure of the quilt.

If you can look beyond color and identify the background, then you can see it everywhere it appears in the quilt. The same is true of the foreground. This is a really helpful skill, especially if you make your quilt in colors different from the ones in the photo.

BACKGROUNDS

The background plays a crucial role in every quilt. I *always* choose it first because it sets the tone for the quilt. A background can be any value from light to dark. It can be any color. You can use a single background fabric as I did in *Pick-Up Sticks* (page 89) or many different fabrics as I did in *Tick Tock* (page 98).

Don't let pieced quilts with lots of colors scare you. Pay attention to the part of the block that defines the design—that is usually the foreground.

Compare the values used in the quilt, rather than the colors. If you have trouble seeing beyond color, make a black-and-white copy of the color photo of the quilt. This can help you see the different values that make up the design, and the background and foreground become more visible.

In my quilt *Goose in the Pond*, the light values make up the block background; the dark values make up the block foreground. I colored the light areas green and the dark areas blue.

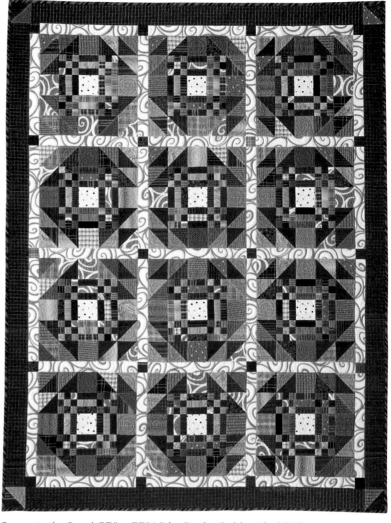

Goose in the Pond, 57″ × 73½″, by Becky Goldsmith, 2007
The background and foreground in a scrap quilt are often different values.

When I made *Goose in the Pond*, I separated my fabrics into a stack of green and a stack of dark blue fabrics (refer to Building Stacks, page 45). There is more variety in the green fabrics, but I made sure that none were as dark or darker than the blues in the blue stack.

When I auditioned a sample block on my design wall, I decided to use a much lighter value in the center square of each block. It adds light to the quilt (refer to Auditioning Pieced Quilts, page 51).

After the blocks were made, I put them back on the design wall and chose the sashing and borders. I stuck to the colors and values present in the quilt. You might decide that you want to add new colors or that you don't need sashing or an outer border. The quilts you make are yours, so you get to be the one to make that decision.

You can make the background and foreground any color you like. You could reverse the values, making the foreground lighter than the background. *The key to success is to be sure to have enough contrast between the background and foreground for the quilt pattern to remain visible.*

FOREGROUNDS

After the background fabric has been chosen, I turn my attention to the foreground. Foreground fabrics need to be different enough from the background to be visible against it. Color and value combinations can be simple or complex.

The foreground of a pieced quilt can often be broken into different parts. The Four-Patches in *Amish Four-Patch* (page 40) have two parts: every block contains two red squares and two blue or green squares. It is easy to see the underlying pattern, and it would be easy to change colors if you wanted to.

The blocks in *Everyday Best* (page 54) look complex, but they are not. I used only fabric with dots in the blocks, separated into light and dark stacks. The darker fabrics occupy the foreground. The little strips in the arcs alternate between light and dark. The fabrics are busy and have a lot of color, but the pattern of the block is discernable.

Stairway to Heaven is a very simple one-block quilt. Each block has three parts. The way the different parts interact is visible only when you see several blocks together. White is the obvious background color because it sits behind, and supports, the fabrics that make up the foreground.

Even though this block looks complex, the arcs break down into lighter background and darker foreground values.

The foreground in this quilt has two parts: the narrow gray strips that imply a shadow and the rainbow-colored strips. In this quilt, the prints are similar in both value and attitude, and that unifies the different colors into the zigzag pattern that dominates the quilt.

Stairway to Heaven (page 106)

The gray and rainbow-colored strips occupy the foreground in this quilt. White is the background.

you are the boss of color

When I design a quilt, I am not working from a pattern or photograph. I don't have a "map" to go by. Sometimes a quilt will "feel" like a particular color to me before I have it all on paper. At other times, fabrics that have been sitting on my worktable for a while wave at me, saying that it is their turn to be used. But one way or another, on the day I need to start cutting, I've decided on the colors I am going to use for that quilt.

When *you* start a quilt, *you* have to decide on the colors that *you* want to use. I wish I could tell you what you like, but really—do you want anyone to have that kind of power over you? Not likely. You do not have to use the colors shown in a pattern. Feel free to change the colors of any quilt you are making—including the quilts in this book.

If you have trouble deciding on colors, my very best advice is to choose at least one color that you really want to work with, and then add to it. Keep in mind what you've read so far, and continue reading.

practical advice

Choosing colors for a quilt does not have to be difficult. I rarely overthink it. Either I am in the mood to work with a particular color or fabric, or the quilt suggests the color to me.

When I made Simply Delicious, *my thinking went like this: fruit goes in the kitchen; kitchens are blue and white. I chose light blue-and-white fabrics for the background. As it turns out, they bring to mind Delft tiles, but that was obvious to me only after the quilt was made.*

Simply Delicious, 54" × 70", by Becky Goldsmith, 2007

I chose blue-and-white fabrics for the background because they reminded me of kitchen colors—and fruit goes in the kitchen.

When I use many different fabrics in a background, I am careful to choose ones that are similar enough in color and value to be read together as background. I keep a close eye on how the different fabrics are working together as I build the quilt on my design wall.

Choosing the colors for fruit in the foreground was equally easy: brown branches, green leaves, red apples, and so on. Again, you might want to play with the colors of the fruit.

HELP—I'VE FALLEN IN LOVE WITH A PHOTO

Quilters often begin a project with a picture of a quilt. You can learn a lot about how to combine colors and values by studying these pictures. However, it is very difficult to reproduce a quilt from a photo *exactly* as it appears in the image.

An often overlooked fact is that the color you see on the printed page—or online—may not be the color of the fabric as it is in the actual quilt. What may look like true blue in the picture could in fact be periwinkle or turquoise.

If you want to reproduce a quilt from a photo, begin with the knowledge that you will be making fabric substitutions. Embrace the fabric hunt. Use the photo as a guide, but pay attention to the fabrics you are accumulating. The colors may be a little (or a lot) different from those in the photo. At some point it's a good idea to put the picture away and focus on how your actual fabric looks together.

—— USING COLORS YOU DO NOT LIKE ——

Have you ever been told that in order to grow as a quilter, you should work with a color that you don't like? I heard that when I was a new quilter, and I accepted that it was true. I became more skeptical as time wore on.

As I set about writing this book, I thought a lot about how I work with color. I always work with fabric that I like. I had never considered making a quilt from fabrics that I didn't choose *and* did not particularly like.

Overall, my palette is made up of colors that are clear and clean. I am comfortable with a wide range of colors and prints inside this spectrum. I rarely use muddy or grayed colors. For example, you won't find Civil War reproduction fabrics in my stash. It's not that these grayed colors are bad—I just don't like them for my own quilts.

Change and challenge can be invigorating, so I decided to challenge myself. I asked readers of my blog to send me small pieces of their ugliest fabric. Some of the pieces I received were not bad, but others ... oh my. It's not just that the motifs printed on the fabrics were odd, but also the horrible mix of colors—from insanely bright to the muddiest grays.

Have you ever seen so much awfulness in one pile of fabric?

My promise was to use every fabric given to me. The question was—how? I tried separating the uglies into dark and light stacks, and it quickly became obvious that that was not going to work—there wasn't enough light fabric to work with.

I changed the rules and allowed myself to add one fabric to use in the background. All the ugly fabric became the foreground, and solid white, the background.

Why white? First, using a neutral background unified the ugly fabrics. White was lighter than all of the ugly fabrics, and it brightened them up. The light-against-dark value contrast allowed the piecing pattern to shine.

Could I have chosen something other than white? Yes. I considered black, dark brown, and charcoal gray, but I knew that the darker uglies would disappear against them. A bright color, such as red, might have been fun—or it could have been a hot mess. I didn't have enough ugly fabric to risk having to start over.

Could I have changed the rules and used more than one fabric for the background? Yes, but it would have made for a much busier quilt. The ugly fabric is busy enough on its own.

Once committed to the white background, I made half-square triangles (page 109) and began playing with them on the design wall.

Everyone needs to use a design wall—including me. I arranged and rearranged the half-square triangles until I settled on the Broken Dishes block (refer to Auditioning Pieced Quilts, page 51).

I had planned to treat this as a scrap quilt, not paying particular attention to color placement. Eventually I realized that I needed to group similar colors together in ribbons across the quilt, which brought order from chaos. After that, it became fun to look at: see *The Ugly Fabric Challenge* (page 60).

The whole experience surprised me. This quilt, which was hard for me to make, has become one of my favorites. The most awful fabrics became my friends and are the most fun to spot.

I realized that there *is* value in expanding your color range—to putting more crayons in your box, so to speak. I still prefer to work with fabric and colors of my own choosing, but the stretch was worth the effort.

TIPS FOR AN UGLY FABRIC CHALLENGE

- Keep the piecing simple and repetitive.

- Cut the ugly fabric into small pieces to hide truly awful designs in the prints.

- A quiet, neutral background can unify wild foreground fabrics.

- Use your design wall. Take the time to play with the pieces on the wall before sewing units together.

- Look at old scrap quilts for inspiration. You may find yourself liking the odd or ugly color combinations you find in them.

- Smile and embrace the unusual.

BUILDING STACKS

I build at least two stacks of fabric for every quilt. The first stack is made up of background fabrics. If I plan to use only one background fabric, this is a very short stack. When I use more than one background fabric, as I did in *Tick Tock* (page 98), I sort the stack by value.

To sort by value, look at the fabrics in front of you and choose the darkest piece. Start the stack with this piece. Continue choosing the next-darkest fabric from the pile and place it on the stack, until the pile is gone. (It is also fine to work from light to dark.)

These are the first background fabrics that I chose for *Tick Tock* (page 98).

If the background has more than one color, I let the colors blend together where possible. In these stacks, the medium gray prints calm down the greenish gold prints that I started with.

The medium gray colors calm down the greenish gold ones.

Next are the foreground fabrics. Focus on the colors, values, and textures that you think might belong in the

quilt. You may or may not use all of the fabrics you put into these stacks, but that doesn't matter at this stage. Don't worry about where a particular fabric might go in the quilt; that comes later.

Brown was the first foreground color that I chose for *Tick Tock* (page 98).

Sort the foreground fabrics by color. You might have a green stack, a red stack, a blue stack, and so on. Sort each of these colors from dark to light.

Place your stacks next to each other on a table or pin them to your design wall. Are the colors working together? Do the background fabrics work with the foreground fabrics? Do you have the necessary light, medium, and dark values to make your quilt? Add and subtract fabric until you think you have enough to begin.

After you have the colors stacked, you can begin to figure out where they will go in your quilt (refer to Design and Audition, page 50).

practical advice

What I have found is that it's easier to work from an organized group of fabrics than it is to work from a disorganized pile. The more you arrange and rearrange the background and foreground fabrics, the more color combinations you will discover, and the easier it will be to get your hands on the just the right color and value when you need it.

These are the stacks of fabric for *Spinning Wheels*, an English paper-pieced quilt. I used a variety of white fabrics in the background and lots of color in the foreground. At this point you don't have to know exactly where each color will go—just that they look good together.

Fabric stacks for my quilt *Spinning Wheels*

practical advice

When you choose one fabric but not another, don't overthink it. If a fabric looks bad in the stack, discard it. If it looks good (even if you're not sure why), keep it in the stack. Don't be afraid to make these decisions.

Each color choice you make helps to define the direction of your quilt. The quilt you build from the colors you chose will be unique.

Remember that you can always add fabric as you are making your quilt and that you don't have to use every fabric in your stack.

Each block in this quilt is made from a different fabric. I didn't know when I pulled the fabrics which ones would be used in the final quilt or where they would be placed. I *did* know that they looked good together.

Spinning Wheels, 36″ × 38″, by Becky Goldsmith, 2013

The fabrics that worked together in the stack work well together in the quilt.

FOCUS FABRICS

In quilting, a focus fabric is a print that has a combination of colors that you like. Some quilters don't use the focus fabric in the quilt at all; they just pull colors from it. The general wisdom holds that if you use colors taken from the print, they will look as good together as they do in the print.

Be aware that the colors in any print do not exist in a vacuum—they influence each other.

Colors are very rarely used in equal amounts in a print. The proportion of each color has an effect on how the colors look. If you change the proportion of the colors and the proximity of one color to another, the relationships between the colors change. If you choose some colors from a print but not others, they will work together differently than they do in the print.

This print, designed by Kaffe Fassett for Rowan Fabrics, would be a great focus fabric.

Many color combinations from this print would work well together, whether they are used with the focus fabric or not. I am particularly drawn to the blues, greens, and orange.

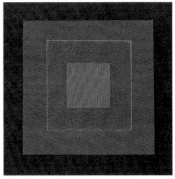

Many wonderful color combinations are possible from the focus fabric.

Some color combinations I would find harder to work with. Although some people would love them, I would have a harder time using these shades of pink, gray, and purple together.

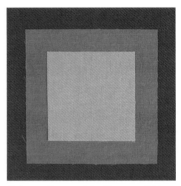

Other color combinations could be a little harder for me to work with.

The moral of this story is that if you use a focus fabric, please don't assume that doing so will always work. Stop to evaluate how your fabrics are looking together—with or without the focus fabric—as you make your quilt.

Targets, a lovely fabric designed by Kaffe Fassett, would be a fun focus fabric.

COLOR DOTS

Have you ever noticed the little color dots in the selvage of fabric? Those dots show the individual colors in the print. Some quilters use these isolated dots of color when they are trying to match individual colors from the print.

Color dots on the selvage show the individual colors that can be found in the prints.

FINDING INSPIRATION

There is inspiration to be found all around you—but it takes practice to pay attention to what you see and, more important, to see what you notice.

Inspiration can strike from out of the blue, or you can plan to be inspired. I love museums—the artwork and the thoughtful spaces always stir my imagination. Nature, books, magazines, blogs, and online content—all of these are sources of inspiration for me. After you find your sources of inspiration, use them.

Great ideas can be forgotten very quickly if you don't figure out a way to keep track of them. I keep journals. They aren't fancy, but they work for me. I also take photos—and I file them in my computer so that I can find them again.

Photo by Heather Robinson

Bondi Blue iMac—love at first sight

You won't use every cool thing that you see, but every now and then something you see will have a big impact on the way you use color. I will never forget seeing the first Bondi Blue–colored iMac in 1998. It was amazing. Every computer up to that point was a lifeless, awful, gray box. And then, color happened to computers!

Then came more candy-colored iMacs. My favorite of these was aqua, which surprised me because at that time I did not like that color. However, that cute iMac made me see aqua blue in a new light. I smile when I think that aqua, a color I never really liked, has become my go-to color.

design and audition

The best way to know if the colors you have chosen are going to work is to audition them on your design wall *before* you begin sewing. If you have ever made a quilt that should have been amazing but wasn't, you probably skipped this step.

Each fabric is auditioning for its role in the quilt. Some fabrics will not make the cut. Others will be perfect. You really don't know until you see them in place on the wall. *You can't fake the audition.* Sticking some fat quarters on the wall and hoping for the best doesn't work.

If I could *make* you audition your quilts, I would. I know that it does take discipline to spend time on the audition process, but trust me, your quilts will be better for it.

— THE CHANGEABLE NATURE OF COLOR —

As you audition your fabric, remember that every color is affected by the color (or colors) next to it. Notice the gray in the plaid fabric in the photo below.

But is the gray in the plaid really gray? When the same plaid is paired with light purple and an off-white print, the gray turns purple.

The soft gray in the plaid is a perfect match to the gray solid.

When the plaid is paired with light purple and off-white, the gray turns purple.

In addition to value, scale, and texture, the color of your fabric is also affected by the context in which it is used. As you make your quilt, you need to be constantly aware of this and pay attention to the way your fabrics are reacting to each other on your design wall.

AUDITIONING PIECED QUILTS

Pieced quilts are harder, but not impossible, to audition. Make a few sample blocks to look at. The more you can place on the design wall, the more likely you are to spot trouble, as I did with my first Square Play blocks.

I spotted trouble during the audition process for *Square Play*.

Square Play (page 70)

The quilt is much happier now.

Although there isn't anything really wrong with these blocks, I thought they looked angry, and my husband, Steve, agreed with me. Anger is not an emotion I like in my quilts, so I softened and moved the yellow fabric. I made the narrow strips aqua. The resulting quilt is definitely happy.

You can design the layout of your quilt during the audition as I did with *The Ugly Fabric Challenge* (page 60). I made all of the half-square triangles for the quilt and then started playing with them on the design wall.

I tried the half-square triangles in a variety of traditional block patterns. It didn't take long for me to realize that the colors looked better when they were grouped together, rather than being all mixed up. I didn't use either of these block patterns, but they pointed me in the right direction.

Photo by Becky Goldsmith

It didn't take long to decide that the half-square triangles look better when like colors are grouped together.

practical advice

Sometimes you see more in a photo than you do when you're looking at the real thing on the wall. Use a digital camera or your phone to snap photos as you work. If you are happy with your color choices, keep cutting and sewing. If a color or value seems off, change it. Keep working at it until you are happy with your quilt.

AUDITIONING APPLIQUÉ QUILTS

When I am making an appliqué quilt, I cut and place every piece of fabric in position on the design wall before I ever take a stitch. By doing this, I *know* that the quilt is going to be wonderful before I put all those stitches into it.

First, place all of the backgrounds on the design wall. If you are going to piece your backgrounds, put as much as you can on the design wall. As you construct background blocks, place them often on the design wall to be sure they are balanced and working well together.

Starting with the first block, trace and cut out the appliqué pieces. Begin with whatever piece seems like the most obvious choice to you. Add the 3/16″ turn-under allowance and cut carefully so that if the piece remains in the quilt, you can use it.

Photos by Becky Goldsmith

Pieced backgrounds from *Tick Tock* (page 98) on the design wall

Tick Tock blocks in progress on the design wall

Work through the quilt until all of the appliqué pieces are on the wall. Place sashing strips, borders—*everything* that is part of that quilt—on the wall.

Are you done? Take a giant step back and really look at it. Take a photo and study it. Begin stitching the appliqué only when you are happy with all of your fabric choices.

practical advice

In the real world, leaves are most often green. When you color an appliqué block, leaves can be any color, but because we are so used to green leaves, green works with just about any floral appliqué design. In fact, green often helps a design with leaves.

Even though the Tick Tock backgrounds are green, the grass-green leaves add a lively spark to this quilt.

subtle considerations

In addition to everything else, there are some subtle things to keep in mind when designing a quilt.

READING A QUILT

English is read from left to right, top to bottom. We are conditioned to look at the upper left corner of a page first; then our eyes track to the right and down the page.

It happens quickly, but I know that I read a quilt in the same way that I read a page. I enter the quilt in the upper left corner. From there my eyes are pulled through to the area with the highest contrast, which is often the focal point of the quilt.

When I am making a quilt, I do pay attention to the upper left corner and to the way my eyes travel over it and then through the quilt.

FOLLOWING LINES

Our eyes follow lines, whether they are in the fabric or sewn into the design of a quilt. We slide along lines until they stop. You can use this knowledge to keep the viewers' eyes moving through your quilt.

I deliberately placed the blue lines in *Pick-Up Sticks* (at right) to keep the viewers' eyes moving into and out of each fireworks-like block.

The lines in *Pick-Up Sticks* (page 89) keep the viewers' eyes moving into and out of each block.

— GIVING THE IMPRESSION OF LIGHT —

The placement of light and shadow adds depth and life to a composition. This is true in paintings, and it can also be true in quilts.

It is not necessary to indicate a light source in every quilt, but when it is appropriate, light and shadow can bring a quilt to life.

Something to Think About

When I cut the rainbow strips for *Stairway to Heaven* (page 106), I also cut a 5½″ × 5½″ square of each fabric. I wasn't sure what to do with these squares until I needed to make the quilt back. You'll have to take my word for it that the squares looked better when grouped by color than they did when randomly placed on the design wall.

The front of this quilt is much more interesting than the back. The zigzag pattern is engaging, and if you are like me, it brings a smile to your face. The quilt back is pretty, but it doesn't hold your attention for long.

It is easy to think that the right combination of fabrics will ensure a terrific quilt top every time—but it doesn't. Fabric alone does not carry the show. I used the very same fabrics on both sides of this quilt, yet the two sides are completely different.

The best quilts combine colors, values, textures, scales, and pattern with a purpose in mind. We can create quilts that are intended to be hugged and loved, to keep us warm, and/or to be admired as art—and every one of them starts with colorful stacks of fabric, sewn with purpose.

Photo by Jim Lincoln for Quilts, Inc.

Everyday Best, 73″ × 73″, by Becky Goldsmith, 2003
The light seemingly glows from the center of *Everyday Best*.

Back of *Stairway to Heaven*

fabric basics

BUYING FABRIC

A quilt shop can seduce you with color. New fabric is likely to attract you first, but be sure to look at the other fabrics in the shop as well—you may be surprised at what you find.

When I shop, I spend more time looking at fabric that is typically "me." However, every now and then I fall for a fabric that is outside of my normal range, which is why I look at all of the fabric in the shop.

Photo by Becky Goldsmith

Colorful fabric on display at Back Porch Fabrics in Pacific Grove, California

Photo by Becky Goldsmith

Solids are an important addition to your stash.

Prints are exciting, but don't forget to look at solids. You need them in your stash.

How much fabric should you buy? I buy more fat quarters than anything else. I buy half-yards of fabric that I know I'll use—dots, some stripes, unusual prints. I buy one-yard cuts of large-scale prints, of fabric that I think I might use for an appliqué background, or for quilt backs and binding. I rarely buy more than a yard of any fabric.

When I am working on a quilt, I work out of my stash. When I run out of a fabric, I am forced to make substitutions. While it can be a challenge, I think that unexpected fabric changes make my quilts more interesting.

TIP

When either Linda or I shop for fabric, we go through and pick up fat quarters in colors that we are interested in. Sometimes we pick up a lot from specific collections, but more often than not, we graze the entire shop. When we have chosen a nice group of fat quarters, we sort them by color to see what might be missing, or we identify fabrics that we want more of. You might try that the next time you shop for fabric.

ORGANIZING YOUR STASH

Quilters find all sorts of ways to sort their fabric. Ideas abound in books and magazines that show quilters' studios. Over the years I have found that shelves work best for me; you might prefer drawers or some other system. There isn't an all-perfect solution—you need to find the way that works for you.

I do think it's best to sort fabric by color. You can also sort each color by value and shade. For example, aqua blues might be on the blue shelf but separated from true blues, and so on. I don't do this myself, but I sometimes wish I did.

My stash lives in our guest room closet. The colors I use the most (blue, green, red, black, and white) each take up a full shelf. Yellow, orange, brown, and purple each take up less than a shelf. I separate woven stripes and plaids from prints on their color shelf. Solids are stacked separately so that I can find them easily. Wools and linens are on their own high shelves.

Photo by Becky Goldsmith

My stash lives in a small 5-foot-wide closet, with floor-to-ceiling shelves.

practical advice

How much fabric do you need? Every quilter has a different answer to this question.

The size of my stash is limited by the size of the closet it lives in. I buy fabric and the shelves get fuller. I use fabric—but not as fast as I buy it. Eventually the shelves overflow and fabric starts piling up on the closet floor. When the piles get deep enough, I weed it out.

Linda taught me years ago that I don't need to keep fabric in my stash that I no longer love. It was hard to accept, but she was right.

How often do you pull fabric from your stash that you can never seem to use? You may remember that you loved it when you bought it. You may even remember how much it cost. But the fabrics that you can never seem to use are just in your way. Donate what you weed out to your guild, have a sale, whatever—just make it go away.

It's hard to do, but I think that once you put a fabric in the "weeds" pile, you'll find that you really don't like it any more. What remains in your stash will be fabric that you love, neatly stacked in place.

FABRIC PREPARATION

If you don't already, please consider washing and drying (called prewashing) your fabric before using it. Why?

Prewash to remove excess dye and chemicals in the cloth. These chemicals can cause an allergic reaction in some people.

Most cotton fabrics will shrink when washed and dried. Different fabrics shrink at different rates; it is better if the fabric has been shrunk to size *before* it is sewn into the quilt.

Fabric off the bolt has a finish that makes it a little slick. Washing removes this finish. In both piecing and appliqué, it is much easier to sew together fabrics that are not sliding against each other.

The seam allowances will fray less as you work with the fabric if you wash and dry your fabric. Frayed edges can be hard to work with.

practical advice

A word of caution: Even if your fabric has been prewashed, it can sometimes still bleed. When I was making Stairway to Heaven *(page 106), my iron spit steam, and two different vintage fabrics with red dots started to bleed.*

It doesn't happen often, but every now and then even a prewashed fabric can bleed.

I was lucky to have the opportunity to replace these two fabrics before the top was quilted and bound, but that is not always the case. The first few times you get a quilt wet, either by washing it or spritzing it with water to remove marks, pay close attention to be sure nothing is bleeding. If it is, be ready to get it back into the washer with the proper washing products. Look online for washing strategies if what you are doing isn't working.

FABRIC REQUIREMENTS

Cotton fabric is usually 40"–42" wide off the bolt. To be safe, all fabric requirements for the projects in this book are based on a 40" width.

Use the fabric requirements for each quilt as a guide, but remember that the yardage amounts can vary depending on how you cut the fabric. My measurements allow for some fabric shrinkage and minor errors in cutting.

BORDERS

This book's cutting instructions are mathematically correct. However, variations in the finished size of the quilt top can result from slight differences in seam allowances. You should *always* measure your quilt before adding borders. When measuring, be sure to measure through the middle of the quilt top, not at the outer edges, which can stretch. Adjust the size of your borders if necessary.

PROJECTS

the ugly fabric challenge

FINISHED QUILT: 52" × 60"

Pieced by Becky Goldsmith. Machine quilted by Angela Walters.

I made this quilt with ugly fabric given to me by quilters who read my blog. Who knew there was so much ugly fabric in the world? Refer to Using Colors You Don't Like (page 44) to read about the fabric I used in this quilt.

The traditional name for this block pattern is Broken Dishes.

MATERIALS

Half-square triangles can be made many different ways, and you are free to use the method you like best. I calculated the yardage using the method shown in Making Half-Square Triangles (page 109). If you use a different method, it may require more fabric and affect the cutting instructions.

- **Ugly fabric:** A variety to total 2½ yards

- **Background fabric (white):** 2½ yards

- **Binding:** ⅞ yard

- **Backing and sleeve:** 3⅞ yards

- **Batting:** 60″ × 68″

CUTTING

Ugly fabric:

- Cut 30 strips 2⅞″ × width of fabric from a variety of fabrics. If your fabric is in small pieces, cut strips 2⅞″ wide × the length available.

Background fabric (white):

- Cut 30 strips 2⅞″ × width of fabric.

Binding:

- Cut 1 square 28″ × 28″ to make a 2½″-wide continuous bias strip 234″ long.

—— HALF-SQUARE TRIANGLE ASSEMBLY ——

1. Make sets of a background strip and an ugly strip, right sides together. From each set, cut 13 sets of squares 2⅞″ × 2⅞″ for a total of 390 square pairs.

2. Sew all the square pairs as directed in Making Half-Square Triangles (page 109).

3. Cut the squares apart between the seamlines.

4. Separate the squares into 2 piles of 390 half-square triangles each.

5. Press the seam allowances in 1 pile toward the ugly fabric. Press the seam allowances toward the background in the other pile. Trim the dog ears.

6. Refer to the quilt assembly diagram (page 62) and place the half-square triangles on your design wall,

alternating the pressed seams. Play with the color placement until you are happy. If necessary, press the seam allowances in the other direction so that the seams nest together.

AUDITION THE HALF-SQUARE TRIANGLES

It may seem like a lot of work to place all of the half-square triangles on the design wall, but it's the best way to see what you've got to work with. View this as an opportunity to play with color. Refer to Design and Audition (page 50).

Take photos of the blocks in different arrangements so that you have a record of what you've done. You may want to go back to a previous arrangement, and having a photo will help.

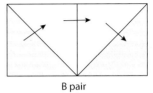
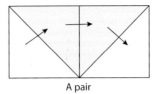

BLOCK ASSEMBLY

Make 98 A blocks, with the background to the outside, and 97 B blocks, with the background to the inside.

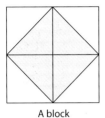
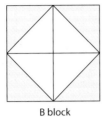

A block   B block

Block assembly—Make 98 A blocks and 97 B blocks.

1. Sew 2 adjacent half-square triangles right sides together into pairs. The diagonal seams will nest together.

2. Press the seam allowances in the direction shown in both the A and B pairs.

A pair   B pair

Press the seam allowances in each pair in the same direction.

3. Refer to the block assembly diagram and sew together pairs to make the A and B blocks. The center seam and the diagonal seams will nest together.

4. Press the seam allowances for the A blocks in the same direction. Press the seam allowances in the other direction for the B blocks.

QUILT ASSEMBLY

Refer to the quilt assembly diagram for construction. Seam allowances are ¼".

SKIP THE ROWS

You could sew half-square triangles together into long rows and then sew those rows together, but that's doing it the hard way. It is faster, more accurate, and easier on the raw edges to sew the half-square triangles together into ever-larger units. You will only have to sew across the quilt once when you join the top unit to the bottom unit.

1. Arrange the blocks on your design wall. Once you are happy with the design, take them off the wall to sew. Be careful to keep them in order.

2. Sew together blocks into pairs. There is an extra block on the right end of the row. Sew this block to the pair next to it. Press the seam allowances toward the B blocks.

3. Sew together pairs into squares. Sew the last set into rectangles. Press the seam allowances in alternate directions.

4. Sew together the units from Step 3 side to side. Press the seam allowances in alternate directions.

5. Continue in this manner—sewing together units into even larger units, pressing the seam allowances in alternate directions—until the quilt is sewn together.

6. Layer and baste the quilt. Quilt by hand or machine.

7. Bind the quilt and add a hanging sleeve, using your favorite method.

Quilt assembly

ode to fred and put a bird on it

FINISHED QUILT: 60″ × 71½″

Ode to Fred: Pieced by Becky Goldsmith. Machine quilted by Angela Walters.

When I travel, I always visit a grocery store. On a trip to Bellingham, Washington, I visited a Fred Meyer store. The floor tiles immediately caught my eye. I especially liked the placement of the small dark squares with the extra-large squares. Both quilts began with this very simple, yet interesting, design.

FINISHED QUILT: 42½" × 51"

Put a Bird on It: Pieced by Becky Goldsmith. Machine quilted by Angela Walters.

The large squares in both of these quilts are the perfect place for a big print. In *Ode to Fred*, the big print is exuberant and colorful, and it is lighter and more airy than the other fabrics. Those more solid, darker squares come forward, putting the big print in the background.

Ode to Fred was so fast and easy to make that I decided to make a smaller version in neutral fabrics.

The fabric used in the same position in *Put a Bird on It* is darker than the other fabrics used in the quilt. The big print itself is legible from a distance, where the designs in the other fabrics have a softer visual texture. In this quilt, the big print comes forward, rather than sitting in the background.

This quilt is very nice without any appliqué. That said, I could not resist putting a bird on it.

You'll notice small triangles on corners of both the large and small squares in *Put a Bird on It*. Where they meet, they form an hourglass. The big prints in *Ode to Fred* were so busy that adding these little triangles would have overly complicated the quilt. However, they spice up the quieter, neutral quilt.

ONE PATTERN, TWO SIZES I made this quilt in two sizes. Rather than reducing the number of blocks, I reduced the sizes of the squares in the smaller quilt. The yardage and cutting instructions for both quilt sizes are listed (page 66). The smaller numbers (in parentheses) are for the smaller quilt, *Put a Bird on It*.

Photo by Becky Goldsmith

Fred Meyer's floor

Fabric note: The big print is Talavera Swirl from the De Leon Design Group for Alexander Henry Fabrics. The berry print used for the large edge triangles is from the Sun-Kissed collection by Michele D'Amore Designs, LLC, for Benartex. Most of the remaining prints were designed by Kaffe Fassett for Westminster Fabrics. Everything else came from my stash.

Fabric note: The big dandelion print is from the Autumn Gatherings collection by Jessie Aller for In the Beginning Fabrics. The print with text used in the large edge triangles is from the Comma collection by Brigitte Heitland, aka Zen Chic, for Moda. The light vertical square fabric is from the Flirt collection by Sandy Gervais for Moda. Everything else came from my stash.

MATERIALS

When you make your own quilt, be sure to use your design wall. Look at the way the blocks are coming together. It is much easier to make changes *before* you have sewn the quilt together.

You could decide to change the values of the fabrics in the B and C squares—making the darker squares run vertically rather than horizontally. I turned the Four-Patch blocks sideways in *Ode to Fred*, which puts the dark squares in vertical rows.

The D and E accent squares can be cut from the same fabric or from two different fabrics. When D and E are the same or very similar in both color and value, a square will form. In *Put a Bird on It*, I chose two fabrics high in contrast, causing an hourglass shape to form where they meet.

I ended up not sewing the small D and E accent pieces into my larger quilt, *Ode to Fred*. That big print is active enough without the added squares.

I didn't intend to add the purple border when I designed *Ode to Fred*, but the quilt needed it.

- **Fabric A (big print):** 1½ yards (⅞ yard)

- **Fabric B (horizontal squares):** 1 or more fabrics to total 1⅛ yards (⅝ yard)

- **Fabric C (vertical squares):** 1 or more fabrics to total 1⅛ yards (¾ yard)

- **Fabric D (horizontal accent triangles):** ¼ yard (⅛ yard)

- **Fabric E (vertical accent triangles):** ¼ yard (⅛ yard)

- **Fabrics F and G (border triangles):** ¾ yard (⅝ yard)

- **Border (optional):** ⅝ yard (½ yard)

- **Binding:** ⅞ yard

- **Backing and sleeve:** 4⅜ yards (3½ yards)

- **Batting:** 68″ × 80″ (51″ × 59″)

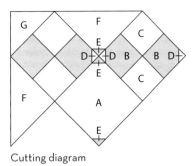

Cutting diagram

CUTTING

Fabric A:

- Cut 5 strips 8½″ × width of fabric (4 strips 6½″ × width of fabric).

  Subcut 20 squares 8½″ × 8½″ (20 squares 6½″ × 6½″).

Fabric B:

- Cut 8 strips 4½″ × width of fabric (6 strips 3½″ × width of fabric).

  Subcut 60 squares 4½″ × 4½″ (60 squares 3½″ × 3½″).

Fabric C:

- Cut 8 strips 4½″ × width of fabric (6 strips 3½″ × width of fabric).

  Subcut 60 squares 4½″ × 4½″ (60 squares 3½″ × 3½″).

Fabric D:

- Cut 3 strips 1¾″ × width of fabric (2 strips 1½″ × width of fabric).

  Subcut 48 squares 1¾″ × 1¾″ (48 squares 1½″ × 1½″).

Fabric E:

- Cut 3 strips 1¾″ × width of fabric (2 strips 1½″ × width of fabric).

  Subcut 48 squares 1¾″ × 1¾″ (48 squares 1½″ × 1½″).

Fabrics F and G:

- Cut 2 strips 12⅝″ × width of fabric (2 strips 9¾″ × width of fabric).

For Fabric F, subcut 5 squares 12⅝″ × 12⅝″ (5 squares 9¾″ × 9¾″). Cut each on the diagonal twice.

For Fabric G, subcut 2 squares 6⅝″ × 6⅝″ (2 squares 5⅛″ × 5⅛″). Cut each on the diagonal once.

Border (optional):

- Cut 7 (6) strips 2¼″ × width of fabric. Sew together end to end.

  Subcut 2 strips 68″ (51″) and 2 strips 60″ (46″).

Binding:

- Cut 1 square 30″ × 30″ (26″ × 26″) to make a 2½″-wide continuous bias strip 273″ (197″) long.

BLOCK ASSEMBLY

1. Sew a B square to a C square. Press the seam allowances toward the darker fabric. Repeat for all the B and C squares.

2. Sew together 2 B/C square pairs to make a Four-Patch. Press the seam allowances in the same direction. Repeat for all the B/C pairs. Make 30 Four-Patches.

Sew together B/C pairs to make 30 Four-Patches.

TAKE A LOOK

This is a good time to place your blocks on the design wall. Check to be sure that you like the placement of the light and dark values in the Four-Patch blocks. Fold the D and E squares in half diagonally and pin them in place. Stand back and look at your quilt. Take a picture. Be sure you like what you see before sewing more.

3. Set aside 12 of the Four-Patch blocks. These are the Four-Patch blocks that are on the left and right sides of the quilt.

NOTE The D and E triangles are sewn in the same manner as the triangles in *Tile Tango*, Block Assembly (page 81).

4. Draw a light diagonal line on the wrong side of all the D squares.

5. Place a D square on a dark corner of one of the remaining 18 Four-Patch blocks, right sides together. Sew on the diagonal line. Repeat for the opposite side of the Four-Patch block. Trim the excess fabric, leaving a ¼″ seam allowance.

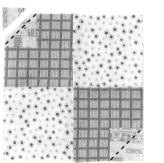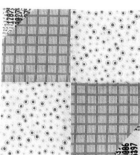

Sew D squares to the 2 dark corners of a Four-Patch block. Trim the excess fabric, leaving a ¼″ seam allowance.

6. Press the seam allowances toward the center of the block. Continue until you have sewn D squares to 18 Four-Patch blocks.

7. Place a D square on a *single* dark corner of each of the 12 set-aside Four-Patch blocks, right sides together. Sew on the diagonal line. Trim the excess fabric, leaving a ¼″ seam allowance. Press the seam allowances toward the center of the block.

8. Draw a light diagonal line on the wrong side of all the E squares.

9. Place an E square on 2 opposite corners of an A block, right sides together. Sew on the diagonal line. Repeat for all the A blocks. Trim the excess fabric, leaving a ¼″ seam allowance. Press the seam allowances toward the triangles.

Sew an E square on 2 opposite sides of the A blocks. Trim the excess fabric and press.

10. Select 8 F border triangles. These are the border triangles on the top and bottom edges of the quilt.

11. Place a D square on the inner point of each of the 8 F border triangles, right sides together. Sew on the diagonal line. Handle the long bias edges carefully so as not to stretch them. Trim the excess fabric, leaving a ¼" seam allowance. Press the seam allowances toward the triangles.

Sew a D square to the inner point of each of the 8 F border triangles. Trim the excess fabric and press.

——— QUILT ASSEMBLY ———

Refer to the quilt assembly diagram (next page) for quilt construction. Seam allowances are ¼".

1. Place the blocks and border triangles on the design wall. Be sure that they are turned correctly so that the D's and E's meet to form squares.

2. Place the F border triangles, right sides together, over the adjacent Four-Patch so that the straight sides match. The pointed ends will extend beyond the edges of the Four-Patch. Sew all the F triangles to the adjacent Four-Patch. Press the seam allowances toward the F triangle.

3. Place the long side of the G border corner triangle on the appropriate Four-Patch. Center the G triangle on the edge of the block and sew it in place. Press the seam allowances toward the Four-Patch.

4. Trim the dog-ears that extend beyond the edges of these blocks.

5. Sew together the blocks into diagonal rows. Press the seam allowances toward the A blocks.

Sew the F and G border triangles to the adjacent Four-Patch.

6. Sew the rows together. Press the seam allowances in the same direction.

7. For *Put a Bird on It*, use the bird pattern (next page) to make a template. Appliqué the bird to the quilt, using the appliqué method of your choice.

8. The outer edges of the quilt may need to be trimmed. Place a 24" ruler over the edge, with the ruler's ¼" line connecting the points of the A blocks. Be sure that the quilt is lying flat and is not pulled out of shape. Trim with the rotary cutter.

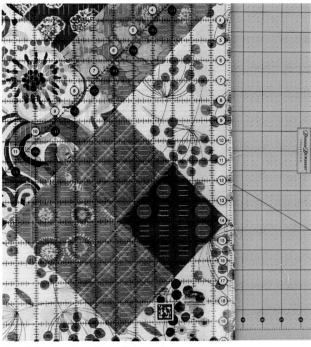

Carefully trim the edges of the quilt.

STAYSTITCH THE EDGES _____

Even though the outer edges of the border triangles are cut on the straight of grain, these edges can be stretchy. To help the quilt keep its shape, machine sew a straight line 3/16″ away from the raw edge. I usually set my machine to sew 8 stitches per inch when staystitching. This is an especially good idea if you are going to appliqué the bird on the quilt.

9. If you are adding the border, sew on the 2 side borders and then the top and bottom borders.

10. Layer and baste the quilt. Quilt by hand or machine.

11. Bind the quilt and add a hanging sleeve, using your favorite method.

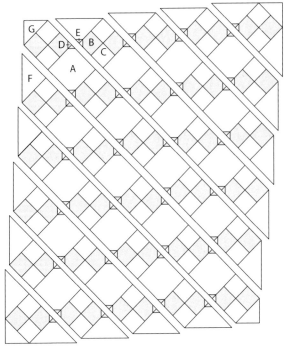

Quilt assembly

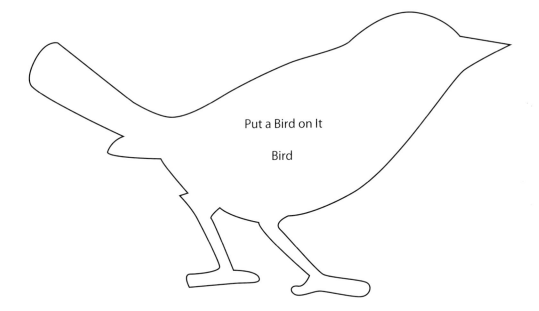

Put a Bird on It

Bird

EASY APPLIQUÉ TEMPLATES _____

To make templates the easy way, use the Essential Self-Adhesive Laminating Sheets from Piece O' Cake Designs (by C&T Publishing). Make enough copies of your pattern so you have a paper shape for each piece that requires a template. For shapes that are stacked on top of each other, you'll need a copy for each shape.

Place the laminate sheet facedown on a flat surface. Peel the backing sheet off, leaving the sticky side up.

Turn your copy facedown and stick it to the laminate. It works best to cup the copy in the center, rather than trying to hold it flat. Cut out each template on the line.

To use the template, place your fabric right side up on a sandpaper board. Place the template right side up on the fabric, and trace. Cut each shape 3/16″ outside the traced line for the seam allowance.

square play

FINISHED QUILT: 50″ × 50″

Made by Becky Goldsmith.

If you want a quilt to be noticed, consider using lots of red. Red is bold. It makes you stop and look. In red, this quilt reminds me of a bandana on a warm summer day.

From the very beginning, I knew this quilt would be primarily red. Red, blue, and yellow form a triadic color scheme (page 13), which helped me to decide on the two accent colors.

My first thought was to make the narrow strips yellow. Refer to Auditioning Pieced Quilts (page 51) to see how that turned out. Luckily, I made a few sample blocks to test the color combination before sewing all of the blocks.

The sample blocks also helped me realize that I needed to do more to highlight the small and medium-sized squares that form when the blocks are sewn together. My solution was to use solid red in the position that creates the diagonal grid. Medium-scale and small-scale prints come together to form distinctive smaller squares.

MATERIALS

Yardage amounts may vary, depending on the number of different fabrics you use.

- **Red solid fabrics:** 1 1/8 yards

- **Red medium-scale prints:** 1 5/8 yards

- **Red small-scale prints:** 5/8 yard

- **Blue accent fabrics:** 1 yard

- **Yellow accent fabrics:** 5/8 yard

- **Straight binding (not bias):** 1/2 yard

- **Backing and sleeve:** 3 3/4 yards

- **Batting:** 58″ × 58″

CUTTING

Red solid fabrics:

- Cut 15 strips 2 1/2″ × width of fabric. Then cut:

    A: 16 strips 2 1/2″ × 16″

    F: 16 strips 2 1/2″ × 10 1/2″

    H: 4 strips 2 1/2″ × 8 1/2″

Red medium-scale prints:

- Cut 21 strips 2 1/2″ × width of fabric. Then cut:

    B: 32 strips 2 1/2″ × 13″

    E: 16 strips 2 1/2″ × 10 1/2″

    G: 24 strips 2 1/2″ × 5 3/4″

Red small-scale prints:

- Cut 11 strips 2″ × width of fabric. Then cut:

    C: 48 strips 2″ × 7 1/2″

Blue accent fabrics:

- Cut 32 strips 1″ × width of fabric. Then cut:

    I: 32 strips 1″ × 14″

    J: 64 strips 1″ × 9″

    K: 24 strips 1″ × 6 1/2″

Yellow accent fabrics:

- Cut 7 strips 2 1/2″ × width of fabric. Then cut:

    D: 48 strips 2 1/2″ × 5 1/2″

Binding:

- Cut 6 strips 2 1/2″ × width of fabric.

SQUARE BLOCK ASSEMBLY

1. Make 2 piles of A strips, each with 8 strips. Set aside 1 pile. Center and sew a blue I strip to each side of the 8 red A strips. Press the seam allowances toward the narrow blue strip.

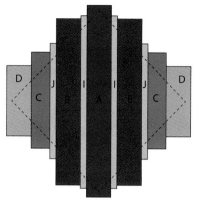

Square block assembly

2. Center and sew a red B strip to each side of the 8 blocks. Press the seam allowances toward the narrow blue strip.

3. Refer to the square block assembly diagram and continue sewing strips to each side of the block. Press all the seam allowances toward the narrow blue strips. Press the yellow D seam allowances toward the D strip.

4. Construct the remaining 8 blocks in the same manner, but this time press the seam allowances toward the red strips.

5. Fold a block right side out to find the center of the A strip. Press each end of the A strip to mark the center. There is no reason to press the length of the A strip. Repeat for all the square blocks.

Press each end of the A strip to mark the center.

6. Place a 12½″ square ruler on the block. Align the diagonal center line on the ruler with the pressed creases in the A strips. You will trim 2 sides of the block. Be sure that the ends of all strips on these sides extend beyond the edges of the ruler.

Center a square ruler over the block and trim 2 edges.

7. Rotate the block. Use the square ruler to trim the block to a 10½″ × 10½″ square in the same manner as Step 6.

RECTANGLE BLOCK ASSEMBLY

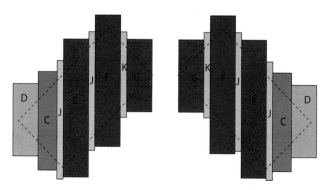

Left rectangle block assembly   Right rectangle block assembly

1. Make 2 piles of D strips, each with 8 strips. Set aside 1 pile to make the right rectangle blocks.

PAY ATTENTION

Refer to the rectangle block assembly diagrams often to be sure that you are sewing the correct strip to the correct side as you construct the block.

2. To construct the 8 left rectangle blocks, center and sew a red C strip to the right side of 8 yellow D strips. Press the seam allowances toward D.

3. Sew a blue J strip to the right side of C, placing the top of the J strip 1" above the top of the C strip. Press the seam allowances toward J.

4. Sew a red E strip to the right side of J, placing the top of the E strip 1½" above the top of the J strip. Press the seam allowances toward J.

5. Sew another blue J strip to the right side of E, placing the top of the J strip 1¼" above the top of the E strip. Press the seam allowances toward J.

6. Sew a red F strip to the right side of J, placing the top of the F strip 1¼" above the top of the J strip. Press the seam allowances toward J.

7. Sew a blue K strip to the right side of F, placing the top of the K strip 1¾" below the top of the F strip. Press the seam allowances toward K.

8. Center and sew a red G strip to the right side of the K strip. Press the seam allowances toward K.

9. Construct the 8 right rectangle blocks in the same manner (Steps 2–7), but this time sew each strip to the *left* side of the previous strip, and press the seam allowances toward the red strips.

10. Fold a block right side out to find the center of the F strip. Press each end of the F strip to mark the center. Repeat for all the rectangle blocks.

11. Place a 6½" × 12½" ruler on the block. Align the 45° diagonal line on the ruler with the pressed creases in the F strips. You will trim 2 sides of the block. Be sure that the ends of all strips on these sides extend beyond the edges of the ruler.

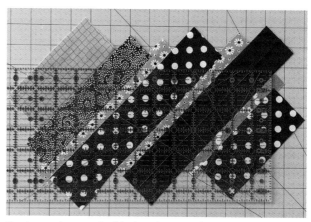

Center a ruler over the block and trim 2 edges.

12. Rotate the block. Use the ruler to trim the block to 5½" × 10½" in the same manner as Step 11.

CORNER BLOCK ASSEMBLY

1. Make 2 piles of H strips—each with 2 strips. Set aside 1 pile. Center and sew a blue K strip to each side of the 2 red H strips. Press the seam allowances toward the narrow blue strip.

2. Center and sew a red G strip to each side of the 2 blocks. Press the seam allowances toward the narrow blue strip.

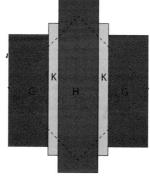

Corner block assembly

3. Construct the remaining 2 blocks in the same manner, but this time press the seam allowances toward the red strips.

4. Fold a block right side out to find the center of the H strip. Press each end of the H strip to mark the center. Repeat for all the corner blocks.

5. Place a 6½" × 12½" ruler on the block. Align the 45° diagonal line on the ruler with the pressed creases in the H strips. You will trim 2 sides of the block. Be sure that the ends of all strips on these sides extend beyond the edges of the ruler.

6. Rotate the block. Use the square ruler to trim the block to a 5½" × 5½" square.

QUILT ASSEMBLY

Refer to the quilt assembly diagram for quilt construction. Seam allowances are ¼".

BE GENTLE WITH THE EDGES

The outer edges of the blocks are cut on the bias and can be stretchy. Be careful as you handle the blocks. Pin gently and don't pull on the edges as you sew.

When you layer and baste the quilt, be sure that the edges are flat and not stretched. Pat down any ripples. I did not staystitch the edges of the quilt because sometimes that can cause the bias edges to stretch more.

Use a binding cut on the straight of grain. As you pin the binding to the quilt, be sure that the edge of the quilt is lying flat. If you see any ripples in the edge, pat them down. Sew the binding to the quilt with a walking foot.

1. Place the blocks on the design wall. Be sure that they are turned correctly and placed so that the seam allowances nest together.

2. Sew together the blocks into rows. Press the seam allowances in alternate directions.

3. Sew together the rows. Press the seam allowances in the same direction.

4. Layer and baste the quilt. Quilt by hand or machine.

5. Bind the quilt and add a hanging sleeve, using your favorite method.

Quilt assembly

opposites attract

FINISHED QUILT: 39″ × 48″

Made by Becky Goldsmith.

This is a fast and very easy quilt to make. It is a perfect gift quilt—for babies, older kids, and grown-ups alike.

You need one background color. White is nice because it disappears and other colors shine against it, but other colors are good choices too. Feel free to choose a different background color. Whatever you choose, put it on the design wall.

I used two complementary colors in the foreground. Complementary colors (page 11) are high energy, and that was the look I wanted. When I built my fabric stacks, I chose orange and blue fabrics in values from light to dark. Refer to Building Stacks (page 45).

It was during the audition process that I decided to shade the quilt from light to dark, left to right. I could have placed the lighter values in the center of the quilt, or at the top or bottom of the quilt, but I liked this placement best.

You could color this quilt in an unlimited number of ways. You could use many colors in the foreground or just one. For a softer look, you could lessen the contrast between foreground and background values. In fact, this quilt goes together so quickly that you might want make it in a variety of colorways.

MATERIALS

ONE PATTERN, TWO SIZES I have included the yardage and cutting instructions to make a larger, 52″ × 64″ version of this quilt. The larger numbers (in parentheses) are for the bigger quilt.

Yardage amounts may vary, depending on the number of different fabrics you choose. Please note that blue and orange fabric strips must be at least 3½″ × 13¼″ (4½″ × 17¼″).

- **White background fabric:** 1⅜ yards (2½ yards)

- **Blue fabrics:** 1 or more fabrics to total ¾ yard (1¼ yards)

- **Orange fabrics:** 1 or more fabrics to total ¾ yard (1¼ yards)

- **Binding:** ¾ yard (⅞ yard)

- **Backing and sleeve:** 3⅛ yards (3⅞ yards)

- **Batting:** 47″ × 56″ (60″ × 72″)

CUTTING

White background fabric:

- Cut 11 strips 3½″ × width of fabric (17 strips 4½″ × width of fabric).

  Subcut 33 strips 3½″ × 13¼″ (33 strips 4½″ × 17¼″).

- Cut 1 strip 3⅞″ × width of fabric (1 strip 4⅞″ × width of fabric).

  Subcut 6 squares 3⅞″ × 3⅞″ (6 squares 4⅞″ × 4⅞″).

Blue fabric:

- Cut 5 strips 3½″ × width of fabric (7 strips 4½″ × width of fabric).

  Subcut 14 strips 3½″ × 13¼″ (14 strips 4½″ × 17¼″).

- Cut 1 strip 3⅞″ × width of fabric (1 strip 4⅞″ × width of fabric).

  Subcut 7 squares 3⅞″ × 3⅞″ (7 squares 4⅞″ × 4⅞″).

Orange fabrics:

- Cut 6 strips 3½″ × width of fabric (9 strips 4½″ × width of fabric).

  Subcut 18 strips 3½″ × 13¼″ (18 strips 4½″ × 17¼″).

Binding:

- Cut 1 square 26″ × 26″ (29″ × 29″) to make a 2½″-wide continuous bias strip 190″ (248″) long.

— PREPARE TO SEW —

1. Separate the white strips into 2 piles. Use a ruler to cut the ends of the strips in 1 pile at matching 45° angles. Cut the ends of the strips in the other pile, angling the cuts in the opposite direction. Discard the triangles.

2. Use a ruler to cut the ends of the orange strips at 45° angles that slant up and to the right. Discard the triangles.

3. Use a ruler to cut the ends of the blue strips at 45° angles that slant down and to the right. Discard the triangles.

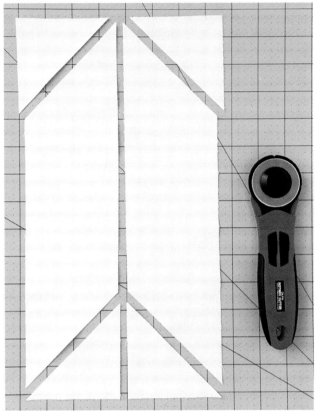

Trim the ends of the white strips at 45° angles—half angling up and to the right, and half angling down and to the right.

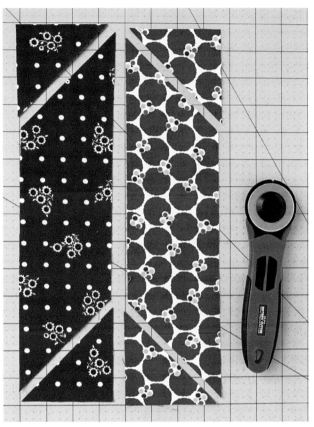

Trim the ends of the orange and blue strips at 45° angles that slant in opposite directions.

BE ACCURATE

Do not shorten the strips. Position your ruler so that the cuts begin or end at the corner of the strip.

4. Cut the white squares in half once, diagonally.

5. Cut the blue squares in half once, diagonally.

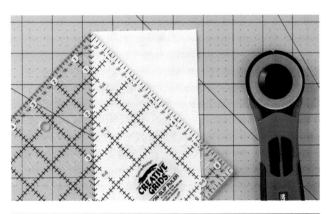

QUILT ASSEMBLY

Refer to the quilt assembly diagram for quilt construction. Seam allowances are ¼".

1. Place the blocks on the design wall. Play with the placement of different fabrics until you are happy with your quilt.

2. Sew together the strips into vertical rows. To do this, place 2 strips right sides together. Offset the ends so that a V is formed at the ¼" seamline. Press the seam allowances toward the dark fabric.

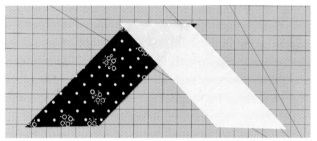

Offset the ends and sew together the strips.

3. Sew the white and blue triangles to the top and bottom of each strip. The points will match on 1 side. The other side forms a V at the ¼" seamline. Press the seam allowances toward the dark fabric.

4. Sew together the strips. Press the seam allowances in the same direction.

5. Layer and baste the quilt. Quilt by hand or machine.

6. Bind the quilt and add a hanging sleeve, using your favorite method.

Quilt assembly

tile tango

FINISHED QUILT: 56″ × 56″

Made by Becky Goldsmith.

On a visit to Santa Fe, I was struck once again by the beauty of the Mexican tiles around the city square. They are beautiful and utilitarian at the same time—in much the same way that a quilt is.

This design is traditional at heart, but it can feel either contemporary or traditional depending on the colors you use. I chose a variety of blues for the flowers and then added purples that blend into the blues. I added orange (the complement of blue) and gold as accent colors. Next came greens for the leaves.

Look at *Pot of Flowers with One Blue Pot* (page 20). The blue fabric (that ought to be green) in the one block really stands out, which is both exciting and quirky. In my quilt, there is one differently colored block, but it is quieter—with less color rather than more color. It asks to be noticed, rather than shouting to be seen (refer to What Do You See?, page 20).

The use of light, medium, and dark values is consistent throughout the quilt, allowing the gray shapes to hold their own visually with the clear colors. I did use some of those gray fabrics in other spots in this quilt. They don't jump out so much because they look grayer in one context than they do in another (refer to The Changeable Nature of Color, page 50).

MATERIALS

- **Block background fabric:** 2 7/8 yards

- **Large A block corner triangles:** 3/8 yard

- **Small B block corner triangles:** 1/2 yard

- **Border background fabric:** 1 yard

- **Large C border corner triangles:** 1/2 yard

- **Small D border corner triangles:** 1/4 yard

- **Appliqué fabrics:** A variety of large scraps, on average 1/4 yard each

- **Binding:** 7/8 yard

- **Backing and sleeve:** 3 5/8 yards

- **Batting:** 64" × 64"

CUTTING

I auditioned all of the appliqué fabrics on the backgrounds on the design wall first. I chose the colors for all of the corner triangles after that. You might want to wait to cut all of your A and B corner triangles until you are sure that they are going to work.

Block background fabric:
- Cut 36 squares 10" × 10".

Large A block corner triangles:
- Cut 3 strips 3" × width of fabric. Subcut 36 squares 3" × 3".

Small B block corner triangles:
- Cut 6 strips 2" × width of fabric. Subcut 108 squares 2" × 2".

Border background fabric:
- Cut 7 strips 4 1/2" × width of fabric. Subcut 52 squares 4 1/2" × 4 1/2".

Large C border corner triangles:
- Cut 4 strips 3" × width of fabric. Subcut 48 squares 3" × 3".

Small D border corner triangles:
- Cut 3 strips 2" × width of fabric. Subcut 52 squares 2" × 2".

Binding:
- Cut 1 square 28" × 28" to make a 2 1/2"-wide continuous bias strip 240" long.

BLOCK ASSEMBLY

Note: If you are doing needle-turn appliqué, add a 3/16″ turn-under allowance to your appliqué pieces.

1. Press the backgrounds. Mark the center of each side on the outside edges of the blocks. Place the backgrounds on your design wall.

2. Using the block pattern (page 83), cut out and prepare the appliqué pieces, using the method of your choice, or see Easy Appliqué Templates (page 69). Place the appliqué pieces on the backgrounds on your design wall. Play with your color and fabric choices until you are happy with the way the blocks look.

3. Audition fabrics for the corner triangles. When you find the right fabrics, cut the squares.

4. Appliqué the blocks.

5. When your appliqué is complete, press the blocks on the wrong side, and trim them to 8½″ × 8½″. The center marks at the edges of the blocks will help keep the appliqué centered.

6. Place the blocks back on the design wall. Make sure that they are turned correctly.

7. Draw a light diagonal line on the wrong side of all of the A and B squares.

8. Place an A square in position at the base of the stem, right sides together. Sew on the diagonal line.

9. Place a B square in position on each of the remaining block corners, right sides together. Sew on the diagonal line.

Place the A and B squares on the block and sew in place.

10. Trim away the excess fabric in each corner of the block, leaving a ¼″ seam allowance. Refer to the quilt assembly diagram (page 82). Press the seam allowances toward the corner triangles in the blue-shaded blocks. Press the seam allowances toward the block center in the unshaded blocks.

Trim away the excess fabric and press as directed.

11. Repeat Steps 8–10 for all the blocks.

BORDER BLOCK ASSEMBLY

1. Draw a light diagonal line on the wrong side of all the C and D squares.

2. Make 3 stacks of border background squares: 4 corners, 24 left border squares, and 24 right border squares.

3. Refer to the border blocks assembly diagram (page 82) and place a C square on a left border background, right sides together. Sew on the diagonal line. Trim away the excess fabric, leaving a ¼″ seam allowance. Press the seam allowances toward the triangle. Repeat for the remaining left border squares.

Place a C square on a left border background and sew in place. Trim excess fabric.

4. Refer to the border blocks assembly diagram (below, at right) and place a D square on a left border background, right sides together. Sew on the diagonal line. Press the seam allowance toward the corner triangle. Repeat for the remaining left border squares.

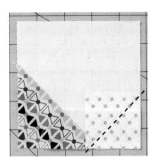

Place a D square on a left border background and sew in place.

5. Make the right border squares and the border corners in the same manner, noting that the squares

are on the opposite corners, and press all the seam allowances toward the center of the squares.

6. Refer to the border blocks assembly diagram and place a D square on a border corner background, right sides together. Sew on the diagonal line. Repeat for all the border corners. Trim away the excess fabric. Press the seam allowances on 2 squares toward the corner triangle, and toward the center of the square on the remaining 2 border corner squares.

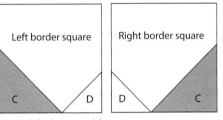
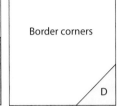

Left border square — C — D
Right border square — D — C
Border corners — D

Border blocks assembly

QUILT ASSEMBLY

Refer to the quilt assembly diagram for quilt construction. Seam allowances are ¼".

1. Place the blocks and border squares on the design wall.

2. Sew together the left and right border squares into pairs. Press the seam allowances in the same direction.

3. Sew a border corner to the adjacent border-square pair. Press the seam allowances in the same direction.

4. Sew a border-square pair to the adjacent block. Press the seam allowances in alternate directions.

5. At the corners, sew the border-square pair and corner strip to the block. You may need to re-press the seam allowances at the corner in the other direction so that the seams nest together.

6. Sew together the blocks into squares. Press the seam allowances in alternate directions.

7. Sew together the block squares into rows. Press the seam allowances in alternate directions.

8. Sew together the rows. Press the seam allowances toward the bottom of the quilt.

9. Layer and baste the quilt. Quilt by hand or machine.

10. Bind the quilt and add a hanging sleeve, using your favorite method.

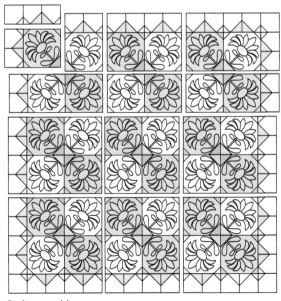

Quilt assembly

Block pattern

say something

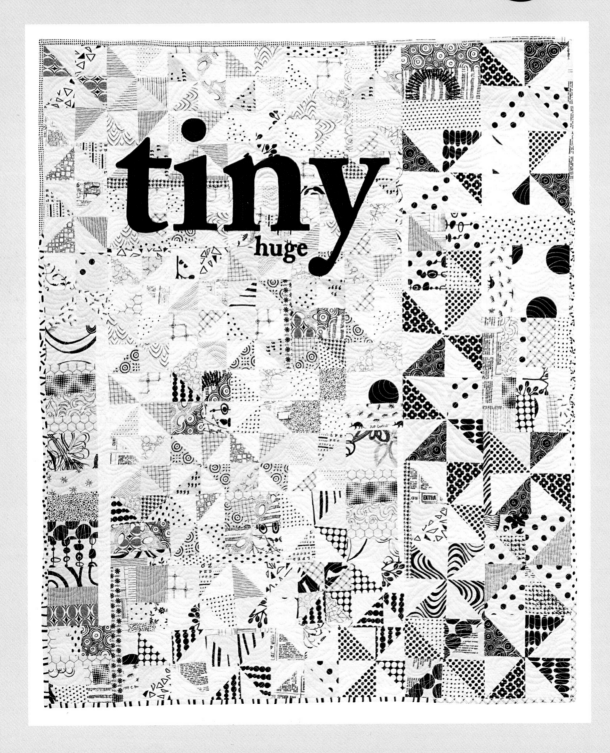

This quilt feels right to me in black and white. The background has the feel of bits of newspaper pages, sewn together—a perfect backdrop for words. I chose a variety of black-and-white and black-and-cream fabrics for this quilt. Some are quiet; others, bold. I was careful with fabrics that might appear to be gray. Refer to About Black-and-White Prints (page 8).

Your quilt does not have to be black and white. Imagine red words on black and white or on a blend of different colors.

No matter the colors you use, be sure to use your design wall so that you can control the values. My quilt is lighter in the upper left so that the very dark words stand out against it.

In addition to paying attention to value, this quilt is also about scale in composition and visual texture (refer to Texture and Scale, page 35).

Shout It Out

We see the words *TINY* and *huge* immediately because they are so dark. But what makes them so engaging is that they *are* words. We read words. In this case, these particular words are even more engaging because the meaning of each word contrasts with its actual size.

I spent a lot of time deciding what word, or words, to put on this quilt. I even wrote a blog post asking for suggestions. I received so many good ones. In fact, tiny/huge was suggested to me by a blog reader (thank you, Sally). Other suggestions were

Bird, Mine, The End, Seed, Grow, Live, Be, Hear, See, Hand, Gave, Life, Tree, Shop, Free, Dang, Cake, Aura, True, Fresh, and more.

Using words on quilts is an interesting way to draw viewers into your quilts. Any word placed on this quilt is going to demand attention. The possibilities are endless! Choose a name, a city, a quotation—something meaningful to you.

Write your word in your own handwriting or use a computer to print it in your favorite font. I used Adobe Caslon Pro, one of my favorite fonts. To do this yourself, print your word on paper as large as you can, and then enlarge the letters on a copier until they are the right size for your quilt. Make a pattern and templates from the enlarged copies.

Construction Notes

The background of this quilt is made up primarily of half-square triangles (page 109) that are pieced improvisationally. I did not use a ruler, so my half-square triangles are not square and their sizes vary. Half-square triangles are set together into pinwheel blocks.

Some areas in this quilt are made from strips of fabric sewn together into short rows. The majority of the pieces in the quilt were cut by eye, with a rotary cutter but without a ruler. The sizes are not precise. The blocks are not truly square. Some blocks are much bigger than others. I added coping strips to blocks that were too small.

WHAT IS A COPING STRIP?

If a block is too small to fit the space, you can sew a strip of fabric to it to make it fit. Coping strips add a quirky charm to this quilt.

Constructing a quilt in this manner is exciting. You are sewing without a net, making decisions based on what you see on your own design wall. It can be a little bit scary, but it is worth the effort.

If you prefer to work with a ruler and precise measurements, I suggest that you make your half-square triangles from squares cut $3\frac{7}{8}$″ × $3\frac{7}{8}$″, which will give you 3″ × 3″ finished half-square triangles. Add some larger half-square triangles and fabric strips for variety.

My quilt is lighter in the upper left and darker on the right and bottom to highlight the words. To achieve a similar effect, be sure to use your design wall as you make your units, and pay attention to the way the values are working together.

MATERIALS

Yardage amounts may vary, depending on the size of your blocks and the number of different fabrics you use.

- **Solid white and very light black-and-white print fabrics:** 1½ yards (I used a lot of solid white and a few very light prints.)

- **Light-medium, medium, and a few dark-medium black-and-white print fabrics:** 1½ yards

- **Solid black fabric for words:** ½ yard (depending on words and font size)

- **Binding:** ⅞ yard

- **Backing and sleeve:** 3⅜ yards

- **Batting:** 50″ × 59″

- **Upholstery vinyl (optional for overlay):** ½ yard

CUTTING

Solid white or very light black-and-white print fabrics:

- Cut a variety of strips of varying widths, between approximately 3⅞″ and 6″ wide. I did not use a ruler.

Light-medium to dark-medium black-and-white print fabrics:

- Cut a variety of strips of varying widths, between approximately 3⅞″ and 6″ wide. I did not use a ruler.

Binding:

- Cut 1 square 26″ × 26″ to make a 2½″-wide continuous bias strip 202″ long.

—— HALF-SQUARE TRIANGLE ASSEMBLY ——

Refer to Making Half-Square Triangles (page 109).

1. Find a light strip and a medium strip that are similar in width and that look nice together. Place them right sides together.

2. Cut the strips into squares. Leave the matching light and medium squares together.

WORK IN BATCHES ——

I did not cut all of my squares at the same time. I cut and sewed half-square triangles in batches. As I made them and constructed pinwheel blocks, I placed them on my design wall. This allowed me to determine the fabric combinations that appealed to me the most. I adjusted the size of my half-square triangles as the quilt grew on the design wall.

3. Make your half-square triangles. The number of half-square triangles that you need will vary depending on the size of the squares you start with. If you cut all of the squares 3⅞″ × 3⅞″, you would need 119 of these matching squares.

Note: If you did not use a ruler, your half-square triangles will not be perfectly square. That's okay.

BLOCK ASSEMBLY

1. Place 4 similarly sized half-square triangles in a pinwheel formation.

Place 4 half-square triangles together to form a pinwheel.

2. Sew 2 adjacent half-square triangles right sides together into pairs. The diagonal seams may or may not nest together. If you need to square up an edge with your ruler, that's fine.

3. Press the seam allowances toward the darker fabric.

4. Using a ruler and rotary cutter, straighten out the inside edge of each pair of half-square triangles.

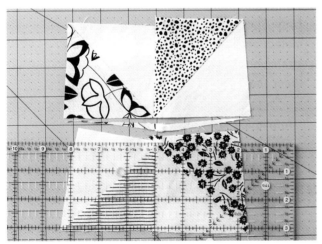

Use a ruler and rotary cutter to straighten out the inside edge of each pair.

5. Sew together the 2 pairs to form a pinwheel.

6. Repeat Steps 1–5 to make more pinwheels.

7. Place the pinwheel blocks on your design wall. Play with their placement. Add large half-square triangle pinwheels and fabric strips for visual texture. Refer to the photo of *Say Something* (page 84) for inspiration.

AUDITION THE HALF-SQUARE TRIANGLES

It may seem like a lot of work to place all of the half-square triangles on the design wall, but it's the best way to see what you've got to work with. View this as an opportunity to play with color. Refer to Design and Audition (page 50).

Take photos of the blocks in different arrangements so that you have a record of what you've done. You may want to go back to a previous arrangement, and having a photo will help.

QUILT ASSEMBLY

Seam allowances are ¼".

I sewed my quilt together in sections, grouping blocks together into rectangular units and the occasional vertical row. Where blocks were about the same size and adjacent to each other, I sewed them together.

1. Place the blocks on your design wall. As you take them off the wall to sew, be careful to keep them in order.

2. Use a rotary ruler and cutter to straighten the edges of the blocks. Sew a coping strip (page 85) to the blocks if you need them to be bigger. If a block is too big, trim it. Press the seam allowances in the direction where they lie flattest.

Use a ruler and rotary cutter to straighten the edges of the blocks. Add coping strips where necessary.

3. Sew together the blocks. Add strips or larger pieces of fabric if you want to. The points may or may not match. Continue to view the growing sections of the quilt on your design wall.

4. Continue in this manner—sewing together units into ever larger units, pressing the seam allowances in alternate directions—until the quilt is sewn together.

5. Square up the outer edges of the quilt if needed.

6. To help the quilt keep its shape while you appliqué the words, sew a stay stitch with your sewing machine 3/16" away from the outer raw edges. I usually set my machine to sew 8 stitches per inch when staystitching.

7. Make your own pattern with the words of your choice. Use a computer font or your own handwriting and enlarge as needed.

8. Make templates for the letters. See Easy Appliqué Templates (page 69). Trace the words onto a piece of clear vinyl for the placement overlay. Draw dashed lines along the center horizontally and vertically.

9. Trace the letters onto fabric and cut them out with their turn-under allowances.

10. Place the letters on the quilt on your design wall. Use the overlay to help with letter placement.

11. When the words are where you want them to be, place a pin in the fabric at each end of both center lines on the overlay. Remove the overlay and letters and press a horizontal and vertical line into the quilt to match the dashed lines on the overlay.

Note: If you pin or baste all of the letters to the quilt at once, you run the risk of them fraying and stretching. It's better to place the letters and stitch them one at a time, carefully.

12. Appliqué the letters to your quilt.

13. Layer and baste the quilt. Quilt by hand or machine.

14. Bind the quilt and add a hanging sleeve, using your favorite method.

pick-up sticks

FINISHED QUILT: 48″ × 48″

Made by Becky Goldsmith.

I love the motion in this quilt. As a kid, I played pick-up sticks. This design reminds me of those colorful piles of skinny plastic sticks. It's also a little like an explosion or fireworks. But no matter what the design reminds you of, this is a fast, fun, and exciting quilt.

The sticks will be more visible against a solid, or quiet, background. If you want to use a print in the background, it is a very good idea to audition it on your design wall. As you can see in this sample block, a print that is too active is very distracting.

Pick-Up Sticks is a good example of how you first notice what is different. The quilt is primarily solid gray, but the gray is not what you see first. The narrow sticks of color are what you see, and the two darkest strips especially catch your eye (refer to What Do You See?, page 20).

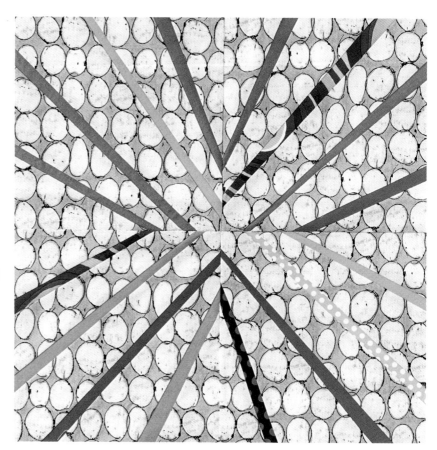

The gray print in this sample block is very active and distracting.

MATERIALS

- **Background fabric:** 2⅞ yards

- **Fabrics for strips:** A variety to total 2½–3 yards

- **Binding:** ⅞ yard

- **Backing and sleeve:** 3⅝ yards

- **Batting:** 56″ × 56″

CUTTING

Background fabric:

- Cut 36 squares 10″ × 10″.

Strips:

- Cut 48–72 strips 1½″ × width of fabric from a variety of fabrics.

Binding:

- Cut 1 square 27″ × 27″ to make a 2½″-wide continuous bias strip 208″ long.

BLOCK ASSEMBLY

AUDITION THE QUILT

While you won't be able to see exactly how these blocks will look when pieced, you can get a good idea by looking at your choices on the design wall first. Place the backgrounds on the wall—this is especially important if you are going to use more than one background fabric.

Cut narrow strips of the "stick" fabrics (¼" to ½" in width). Place them on the backgrounds to mimic how they will look in the quilt. Take a photo if that will help you to see how your color choices will look. These audition strips are not included in the yardage totals.

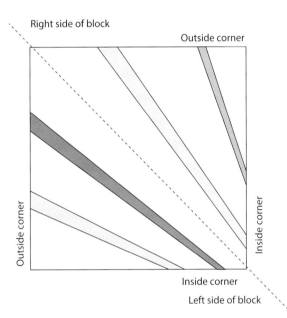

Block diagram

The block is divided into 2 halves along a diagonal axis. Each half has an inside edge and an outside edge. The angle of each strip varies, but in general, the bases of the strips are closer to the inside corner of the block. The outer ends of the strips tend to be closer to the outside corners of the block.

The piecing goes faster if you construct 4 blocks at a time. Keep these 4 blocks together during the piecing process. After all of your blocks are made, mix them up in the quilt.

1. Place 4 background squares right side up in a stack on your cutting mat. If this is a fabric with a directional print, be sure to rotate half of the blocks once, counterclockwise, before you begin cutting.

2. Place a rotary ruler on top of the stack in position to make the cut for the strip on the far left side of the block. Cut through the stack with a rotary cutter. Separate the 2 block stacks.

3. Place 4 strips right side up in a stack between the 2 sides of the block, closer to the large side.

Trim each end of the strip stack 1" longer than the outer edges of the larger side of the block.

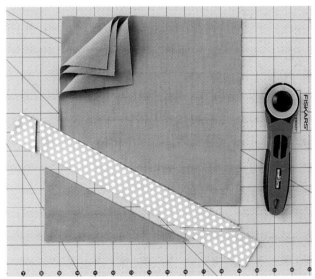

Trim each end of the strip stack 1" longer than the edges of the block.

4. Center the top strip right sides together over the top triangle. Sew the strip to the triangle. Repeat this step for the remaining strips and triangles. Press the seam allowances away from the strip.

5. Place 1 triangle/strip unit on your cutting mat. Trim the strip at an angle, leaving ³/₈″ to ⁷/₈″ of the strip. Discard the excess strip fabric. Repeat this step for all the triangle/strip units, trimming the strips at varying widths and angles one at a time.

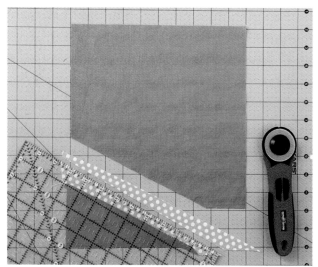

Trim each strip at varying widths.

6. Center a triangle/strip unit right sides together over the body of the block. Sew together the 2 sides of the block. Repeat this step for the remaining pieces. Press the seam allowances away from the strip.

7. Stack the blocks on your cutting mat, lining up the edges on the top and right sides of the block. The strips and the edges on the bottom and left sides of the block are not going to match up.

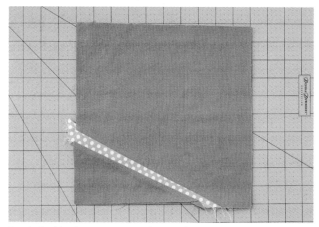

Stack the blocks on your mat, aligning the edges on the top and right sides.

8. Decide where you want the next strip to be and cut through the stack. Separate the 2 block stacks. Repeat Steps 2–7 until you have 4 strips in each block.

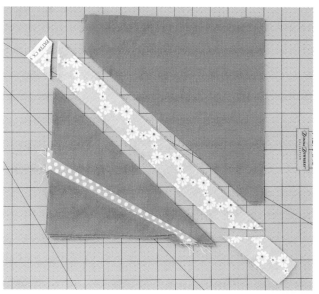

Stack the blocks and make the cut for the next strip. Repeat Steps 2–7.

9. Place a block right side up on your cutting mat. Trim it to 8½″ × 8½″. Repeat for all blocks.

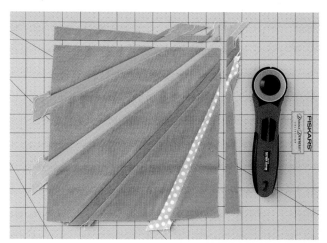

Trim each block to 8½″ × 8½″.

10. Turn each block over and trim away the dog-ears on each edge of the block.

11. Repeat for all the blocks.

Trim away the dog-ears on the back of the block.

QUILT ASSEMBLY

Refer to the quilt assembly diagram for quilt construction. Seam allowances are ¼".

1. Sew together the first 2 pairs of blocks. Press the seam allowances in the same direction, as shown. Sew together these 2 pairs to make 1 larger block. Press the seam allowances in the same direction around the center of the block as indicated.

2. Turn the block over and open the seams at the center of the block so that they lie flat. Press.

3. Construct 8 more large blocks.

4. Sew together the blocks into rows. Press the seam allowances in alternate directions.

5. Sew together the rows. Press the seam allowances toward the bottom of the quilt.

6. Layer and baste the quilt. Quilt by hand or machine.

7. Bind the quilt and add a hanging sleeve, using your favorite method.

Press the seam allowances in the same direction around the center of the block.

Quilt assembly

box of rain

This quilt is all about the interplay of clear colors and gray colors. Clear colors come forward, and grays tend to recede; that is very evident in this quilt. Refer to Clarity (page 31). I don't own many grayed fabrics, but I did have a selection of gray-blues in my stash, which is why my quilt is blue.

Your quilt can be any color. And even though I was excited by the combination of clear and gray colors, you don't have to be. Your quilt can be made from lights and darks in one or more colors.

MATERIALS

Yardage amounts may vary, depending on the number of different fabrics you choose.

I substituted 3 yellow squares for darker blue ones to add a bit of light to the composition. That yardage is not included below.

- **Light gray background fabrics:** 1 or more fabrics to total 1¼ yards
- **Darker clear blue fabrics:** 1 or more fabrics to total 1¼ yards
- **Binding:** ¾ yard
- **Backing and sleeve:** 3¼ yards
- **Batting:** 48″ × 56″

CUTTING

Light gray background fabrics:
- Cut 16 strips 2½″ × width of fabric.

  Subcut 120 squares 2½″ × 2½″.

  Subcut 60 strips 2½″ × 4½″.

Darker clear blue fabrics:
- Cut 16 strips 2½″ × width of fabric.

  Subcut 120 squares 2½″ × 2½″.

  Subcut 60 strips 2½″ × 4½″.

Binding:
- Cut 1 square 26″ × 26″ to make a 2½″-wide continuous bias strip 192″ long.

—— LIGHT GRAY BLOCK ASSEMBLY ——

1. Separate the light gray squares into 2 piles of 60 each.

2. Place a pair of squares on the table with the light gray square above the darker blue square. Position a matching 4½″ light gray strip to the left of the pair of squares. This orientation is important.

3. Sew a darker clear blue square to each light gray square. Press the seam allowances toward the darker blue fabric. Sew the pieced squares to the gray strip. Press the seam allowances toward the gray strip. Repeat Steps 2 and 3 for the remaining 59 light gray squares in the first stack.

Position a 4½″ light gray strip to the left of the pair of squares and sew them together.

4. Arrange 4 squares together with the darker blue to the inside of the block. Sew the squares together into rows. Press the seam allowance in the top row to the left and the bottom row to the right.

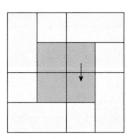

Sew 4 squares together into 2 rows. Press as shown.

5. Sew together the 2 rows. Press the seam allowance toward the bottom of the block.

6. Repeat Steps 4 and 5 to make a total of 15 light gray blocks.

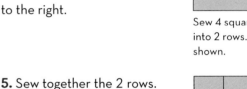

Sew together the 2 rows. Press as shown.

— DARKER CLEAR BLUE BLOCK ASSEMBLY —

1. From the second pile of gray squares, place a pair of squares on the table with the darker blue fabric above the light gray. Position a matching 4½″ darker blue strip to the left of the pair of squares. This orientation is important.

2. Sew a darker clear blue square to a light gray square. Press the seam allowances toward the darker blue fabric.

3. Sew the pieced squares to the blue strip. Press the seam allowances toward the blue strip. Repeat Steps 1–3 for the remaining 59 light gray squares.

Position a 4½″ darker blue strip to the left of the pair of squares and sew them together.

4. Arrange 4 squares together with the light gray to the inside of the block. Sew the squares together into rows. Press the seam allowance in the top row to the left and the bottom row to the right.

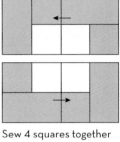

Sew 4 squares together into 2 rows. Press as shown.

5. Sew together the 2 rows. Press the seam allowance toward the top of the block.

6. Repeat Steps 4 and 5 to make a total of 15 darker clear blue blocks.

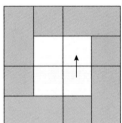

Sew together the 2 rows. Press as shown.

QUILT ASSEMBLY

Refer to the quilt assembly diagram for quilt construction. Seam allowances are ¼".

1. Place the blocks on the design wall. Play with the placement of the blocks until you are happy with your quilt.

2. Sew together the blocks into rows. Press the seam allowances of the rows in alternate directions.

3. Sew together the rows. Press the seam allowances in the same direction.

4. Layer and baste the quilt. Quilt by hand or machine.

5. Bind the quilt and add a hanging sleeve, using your favorite method.

Quilt assembly

tick tock

FINISHED QUILT: 61" × 61"

Made by Becky Goldsmith.

This quilt began with the purchase of a half-yard piece of green linen fabric featuring retro clocks designed by Melody Miller for Kokka. I added greenish golds and yellows to go with the clock print in the background. Refer to Building Stacks (page 45) to see my stack of background fabrics. Also refer to Auditioning Appliqué Quilts (page 52).

Overall, the background colors are less clear than the colors in the foreground, which helps to bring the appliqué forward. The colors and textures in the background, while busy, are enough alike to be read together as background (refer to The Structure of a Quilt, page 39).

This quilt also uses contrast of visual textures and scales. There is a lot going on in the background (refer to Texture and Scale, page 35)—so much that the background could almost have stood alone.

The appliqué shapes need to be big, and the biggest shapes need to be cut from fabrics that are solid or near-solid in order to be visible against the busy background. Using similar colors in each block for the same shape also makes the pattern legible—I tried using multiple flower colors during the design phase and the results were not good—a good lesson in the value of using a design wall, especially when improvising.

The appliqué pattern in the border—which is a much larger version of the appliqué pattern in each block—frames the quilt and emphasizes the design of the blocks.

Because my quilt is improvisationally constructed, I didn't use a ruler, and no block is like another. My blocks are not truly square, nor are they identical in size.

If you prefer to follow a pattern, I have included measurements and pattern pieces that you can use to create square blocks and a square quilt.

I improvised the appliqué shapes in my quilt. The flowers and leaves were cut individually, by eye, which gives my quilt a more whimsical look. You have the choice of doing the same or following the patterns provided.

MATERIALS

Yardage amounts may vary, depending on how you piece your quilt and the number of different fabrics you use. Read through all of the instructions for this project before proceeding.

- **Block background fabrics:** 2½ yards

- **Border background fabrics:** 1⅞ yards

- **Appliqué fabrics:** A variety of large scraps, fat quarters, or larger pieces in a variety of colors for the flowers, stems, and leaves

- **Stem fabric (optional, for all stems from one fabric):** ¼ yard

- **Sashing fabrics:** ⅜ yard

- **Binding:** ⅞ yard

- **Backing and sleeve:** 4⅜ yards

- **Batting:** 69″ × 69″

- **Notions:** *Packages of precut papers are available at pieceocake.com.*

  ½″ hexagon paper pieces: You will need 252 individual hexagons.

  1″ hexagon paper pieces: You will need 28 individual paper hexagons.

  Upholstery vinyl (optional, for overlay,): ½ yard

CUTTING

You can use the measurements below for precise cutting or cut improvisationally.

Block background fabrics:

- Cut or construct 9 squares 16″ × 16″.

Border background fabrics:

- If you are using 1 border background fabric, cut the following from the lengthwise grain of the fabric:

  D: 4 strips 3¼″ × 47″

  F: 4 strips 6¾″ × 47″

- **For improvisational piecing:** Construct 4 strips approximately 10″ × 47″.
  Note: Be sure to cut the D strips from the inside edges of each strip. Keep the D and F strips from each border strip together.

- **G:** Cut or construct 4 squares 8½″ × 8½″ (border corners).

Stem fabric for borders:

- Cut 5 strips 1″ × width of fabric.

  E: From these strips, construct 4 strips 1″ × 47″.

- **For improvisational piecing:** Cut and construct 4 strips approximately 1″ × 47″.

Sashing fabrics:

- Cut 9 strips 1¼″ × width of fabric.

  A: Subcut 6 strips 1¼″ × 14½″.

  B: Construct 4 strips 1¼″ × 44″.

  C: Construct 2 strips 1¼″ × 45½″.

- **For improvisational piecing:** Cut and construct A, B, and C strips to approximately the sizes listed above.

Binding:

- Cut 1 square 29″ × 29″ to make a 2½″-wide continuous bias strip 280″ long.

BLOCK ASSEMBLY

Note: If you are doing needle-turn appliqué, add a 3/16″ turn-under allowance to your appliqué pieces.

1. Cut or construct the block backgrounds.

2. Press the backgrounds. If you like, mark the center of each side on the outside edges of the blocks. Place the backgrounds on your design wall.

3. Make the hexagon flower centers using the method of your choice. I used English paper piecing.

4. Choose 2 fabrics for each flower's appliqué pieces.

To follow the drawn pattern:

Make 4 copies of the flower block pattern (page 104) and tape them together. Cut out and prepare the appliqué pieces, using the method of your choice. If you choose to use the vinyl overlay to aid in the flower placement, trace the flower, stem, and leaves onto the vinyl.

To improvise the flowers:

Choose 2 fabrics to make 1 flower. Place a piece of fabric for a scalloped inner flower right side up on a sandpaper board (refer to Using a Sandpaper Board, below). Place a pieced flower center on this fabric. Draw a scalloped flower shape around the flower center.

Draw a scalloped flower shape around the flower center.

Cut out the scalloped flower, including a 3/16″ turn-under allowance if needed. Place it on top of the fabric for the bottom of the flower, everything right side up. Trace a circular shape around the scalloped flower.

Cut out the rounded flower shape, including a 3/16″ turn-under allowance if needed. Repeat for all the flowers.

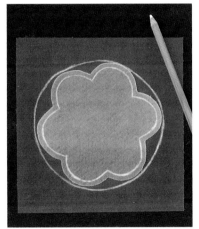

Trace a circular shape around the scalloped flower.

USING A SANDPAPER BOARD

When drawing or tracing on fabric, put the fabric on a sandpaper board to keep the fabric from shifting around as you draw or trace. I like to use the Essential Sandboard from Piece O' Cake Designs (by C&T Publishing).

To improvise the stems and leaves:

Use your scissors or rotary cutter and cut the shapes by eye. Be sure to include a 3/16″ turn-under allowance, if needed. You can refer to the pattern for sizing. These shapes will not have any chalk lines on them because you are not tracing a template.

5. Place the appliqué pieces on the backgrounds on your design wall. Use the overlay to place the appliqué pieces in the proper position, or, if you are improvising, place them by eye.

6. Play with your color and fabric choices until you are happy with the way the blocks look.

7. Appliqué the blocks.

8. When your appliqué is complete, press the blocks on the wrong side. If you are following the pattern, trim them to 14½″ × 14½″. If you are improvising, trim them to the size that works for you.

9. Place the blocks back in position on the design wall.

SASHING

As you work on the blocks, you may begin to have an idea of what will work for the sashing. I often place test strips on my design wall as I am working on the blocks and/or borders to see what might work.

After you decide on the right fabric for the sashing, cut the strips and place them on the design wall.

BORDER ASSEMBLY

Choose your method for Steps 1–4.

To follow the pattern:

Refer to the quilt assembly diagram (next page).

1. Cut or construct the D and F border strips.

2. Sew an E stem strip between a D and F border strip. Press the seam allowances toward the E stem strip.

3. Repeat Steps 1 and 2 for all the borders.

4. Cut out the border leaves and flowers using the patterns (pages 104 and 105). See Easy Appliqué Templates (page 69). *Note: Cut a total of 44 leaves using the patterns provided, making an assortment of sizes.*

To improvise the borders:

1. Construct 4 border strips that are approximately 10″ × 47″.

2. Cut each border strip, referring to the measurements for the D and F strips to help you decide where to cut your border backgrounds.

3. Sew an E stem strip between a D and F border strip. Press the seam allowances toward the E stem strip. Repeat for all the borders.

4. Cut the leaves and flowers for the borders by eye. Follow Block Assembly, Step 3 (page 101) to make the hexagon flower. You can refer to the patterns for the leaves and flowers (pages 104 and 105) for help with sizing.

For either method, continue with Steps 5–8.

5. Place the appliqué pieces on the border backgrounds on your design wall. The leaves in the borders are positioned by eye. Refer to the quilt photo (page 98).

Play with your color and fabric choices until you are happy with the way the borders look.

6. After the leaves are where you want them, pin and then baste the leaves to each border. Set the flowers for the border corners aside for now.

7. Appliqué the leaves to each border.

8. When your appliqué is complete, press the borders on the wrong side. If you are following the pattern, trim the borders to 8½″ × 45½″. If you are improvising, wait to trim the borders.

QUILT ASSEMBLY

Refer to the quilt assembly diagram for quilt construction. Seam allowances are ¼″.

NOTE **If you are improvising:** You will probably need to trim the edges of the blocks, sashing, and borders where they meet. Overlap these edges with right sides up, and cut them to match before sewing them together.

1. Place the blocks, sashing strips, borders, and border corners G on the design wall.

2. Sew the A strips between the adjacent blocks in each row. Press the seam allowances toward the sashing.

3. Sew the B strips between the rows and at the top and bottom of the quilt center. Press the seam allowances toward the sashing.

4. Sew the C strips to each side of the quilt center. Press the seam allowances toward the sashing.

NOTE **If you are improvising:** Trim the border strips to fit your quilt center. Add fabric to the strips as necessary.

5. Sew the side borders to the quilt. Press the seam allowances toward the sashing.

6. Sew the border corners to each end of the top and bottom borders. Press the seam allowances toward the border corners G.

7. Sew the top and bottom borders to the quilt. Press the seam allowances toward the sashing.

8. Make 4 border corner flowers using the pattern (page 105) and the same method as Block Assembly, Steps 3 and 4 (page 101). Appliqué the flowers to the quilt corners.

9. Layer and baste the quilt. Quilt by hand or machine.

10. Bind the quilt and add a hanging sleeve, using your favorite method.

Quilt assembly

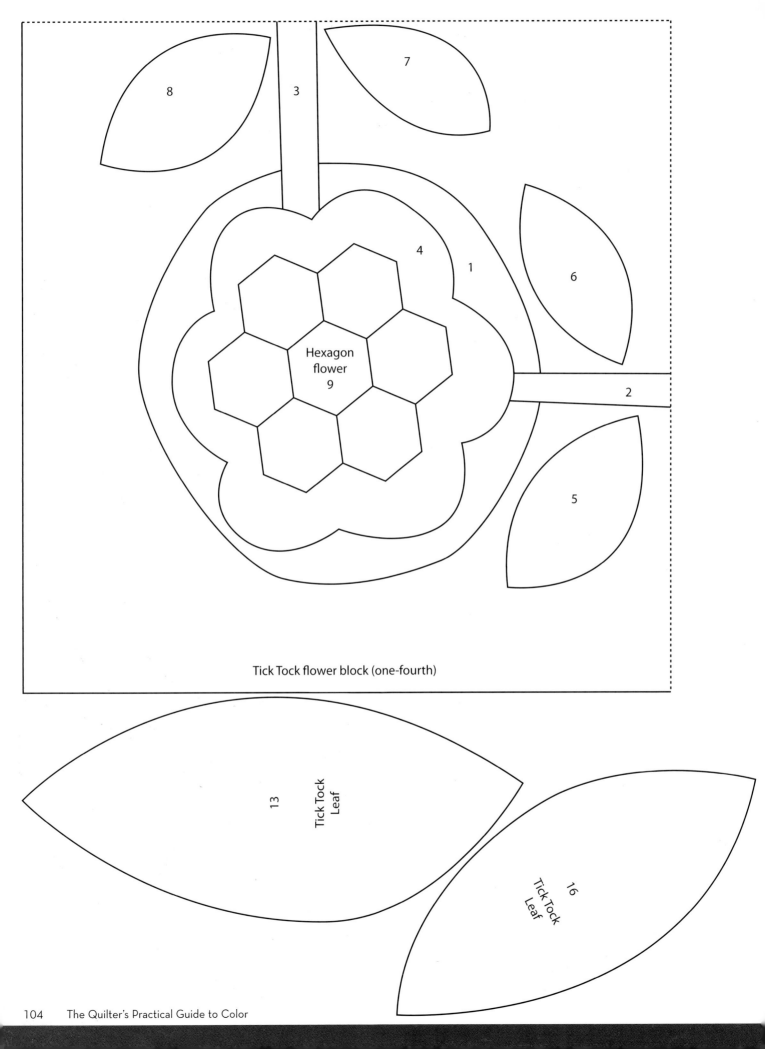

Tick Tock flower block (one-fourth)

8

3

7

4

1

6

Hexagon
flower
9

2

5

13

Tick Tock
Leaf

16

Tick Tock
Leaf

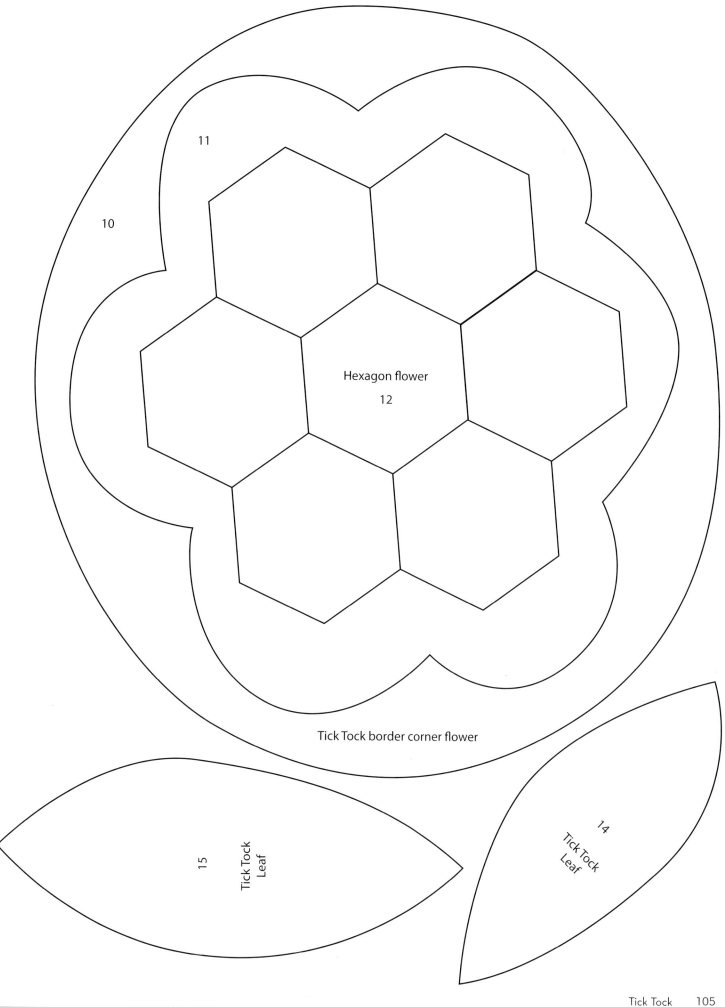

11

10

Hexagon flower

12

Tick Tock border corner flower

15

Tick Tock
Leaf

14

Tick Tock
Leaf

stairway to heaven

FINISHED QUILT: 43½″ × 48½″

Made by Becky Goldsmith.

I love this quilt, not because it was hard to make or incredibly inventive—the pattern is traditional and it is simple to sew. What I love is the way the colors blend into each other and the depth that comes from the shadowlike strips of gray.

This is a quilt with three parts: background, shadow, and foreground. My foreground is made up of rainbow fabrics. Using one white fabric (the background) and one gray fabric (the shadow) simplifies the quilt, keeping it from feeling visually cluttered. The white and gray strips give the quilt a structure that can be read at a glance, leaving you free to enjoy the colors and patterns in the other fabrics (refer to The Structure of a Quilt, page 39).

This quilt has 72 blocks. I chose 72 different light prints to make up my rainbow. When I built the fabric stacks, I had no idea where the different colors would go.

After my blocks were made, I did what I've asked you to do … I played with their placement on my design wall.

It is a good idea to take photos of the blocks in different arrangements, just in case you want to go back. Your design wall doesn't have an Undo button! :-)

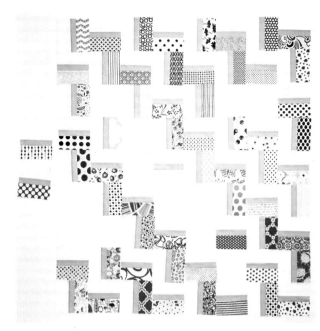

Colors need to be grouped together to get a rainbow effect.

MATERIALS

Yardage amounts may vary, depending on the number of different fabrics you choose.

- **White fabric:** 7/8 yard

- **Solid gray fabric for blocks and border:** 7/8 yard

- **Assortment of rainbow fabrics:** 1 or more fabrics to total approximately 1 yard

- **Binding:** 7/8 yard

- **Backing and sleeve:** 3 3/8 yards

- **Batting:** 51″ × 56″

CUTTING

White fabric:

- Cut 11 strips 2½″ × width of fabric.

Solid gray fabric for blocks:

- Cut 11 strips 1½″ × width of fabric.

Solid gray fabric for border:

- Cut 6 strips 2″ × width of fabric.

Rainbow fabrics:

- Cut 72 strips 2½″ × 5½″ from a variety of fabrics.

Binding:

- Cut 1 square 26″ × 26″ to make a 2½″-wide continuous bias strip 194″ long.

BLOCK AND BORDER ASSEMBLY

1. Sew a white strip to a gray strip. Press the seam allowances toward the gray fabric. Repeat for all the strips.

2. Cut 72 white/gray strips 5½" long from the pieced strips.

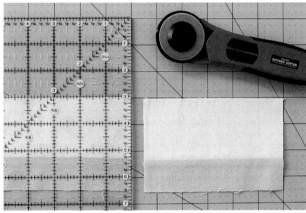

Cut 72 white/gray strips 5½" long from the pieced strips.

3. Sew a rainbow strip to the gray fabric in each block. Press the seam allowances toward the rainbow fabric.

4. Repeat Steps 2 and 3 to make a total of 72 blocks.

5. Sew gray border strips together and cut 2 strips 2" × 45½" for the sides and 2 strips 2" × 43½" for the top and bottom.

Sew a rainbow strip to the gray fabric in each block.

QUILT ASSEMBLY

Refer to the quilt assembly diagram for quilt construction. Seam allowances are ¼".

1. Place the blocks on the design wall. Play with the placement of the blocks until you are happy with your quilt.

2. Sew together the blocks into rows. Press the seam allowances toward either the white or rainbow 5½" strips.

3. Sew together the rows. Press the seam allowances in the same direction.

4. Sew the side borders on either side. Press the seams toward the borders.

5. Add the top and bottom borders. Press the seams toward the borders.

6. Layer and baste the quilt. Quilt by hand or machine.

7. Bind the quilt and add a hanging sleeve, using your favorite method.

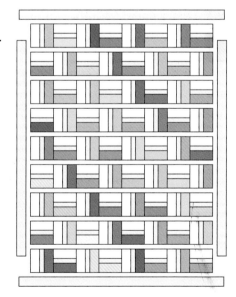

Quilt assembly

appendix

—— MAKING HALF-SQUARE TRIANGLES ——

This is a fast and efficient way to make half-square triangles. If you cut and sew accurately, you will love the results.

If you prefer to make half-square triangles using a different method, you can certainly do that. Regardless of the method you use, it is a good idea to make a few to test for size first. Then cut and sew the number required in the pattern.

1. Follow the instructions in each pattern and cut the required number of squares.

2. Cut an 8″ strip of colored painter's tape. Place the left edge of the tape on the ¼″ guide on the throat plate, to the right of the needle. Stick the tape to your sewing machine bed and to the table, both behind and in front of the needle, as shown in the photo below. Do your best to keep the tape perpendicular to the edge of the table (not at a slant).

Place the edge of the colored tape ¼″ to the right of your sewing machine needle, perpendicular to the edge of the table.

3. Place 2 fabrics that make up a half-square triangle right sides together. With the background on top, place 2 opposite points on the left side of the tape.

Place 2 opposite points of a half-square triangle pair on the left side of the tape.

4. Sew, being sure to keep the points on the line marked by the left side of the tape. Once you have started sewing, keep your eyes on the point in front of the needle, letting it follow the edge of the tape.

Sew, keeping the points on the line at the edge of the tape. Keep your eyes on the point in front of the needle, keeping it on the edge of the tape.

5. Sew all the pairs of squares in this manner, chaining them together.

Sew all the pairs, chaining them together.

6. Remove the squares from the machine. I prefer to cut them apart but you can leave the chain intact if that works better for you.

7. Turn the squares. Place the same points on the edge of the tape and sew down the other side, 1/2" away from the first seam. Let the points follow the left edge of the tape as you did in Step 4. Sew all the square pairs, chaining them together.

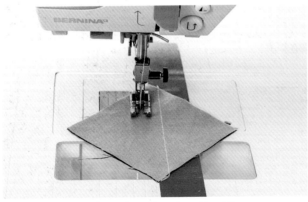

Turn the squares and sew down the other side of the square. Repeat for all the squares.

8. Remove the squares from the machine and cut them apart.

9. Use a rotary cutter and ruler to cut the squares apart between the seamlines.

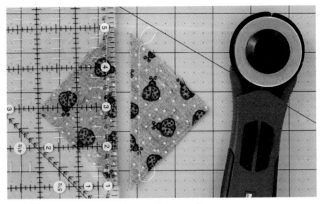

Cut the squares apart between the seamlines.

10. Follow the instructions in the pattern and press the seam allowances in one direction or the other.

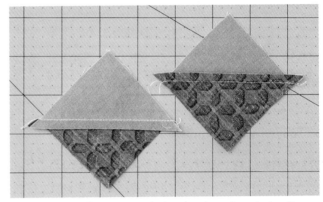

Press the seam allowances as directed in the pattern instructions.

11. Trim the dog-ears even with the raw edge of the half-square triangles. Use your rotary ruler and cutter to square up the half-square triangles if necessary.

Trim the dog-ears and square up the half-square triangles as needed.

ABOUT THE AUTHOR

Photo by Chad Mahlum Photography

Becky Goldsmith

Becky grew up in Oklahoma and met her husband, Steve, at the University of Oklahoma. They married in 1978, at the end of their senior year. Steve is a college professor and Dean of the Sciences at Austin College in Sherman, Texas.

Their two sons, Chris and Jeff, are grown and married to Lorna and Celia, respectively. Becky and Steve are having great fun watching their grandchildren, Elanor, Jack, and Bear, grow up.

Becky met Linda Jenkins, her partner in Piece O' Cake Designs, not long after she started quilting, at a meeting of the Green Country Quilters' Guild in Tulsa. They've been friends ever since. They started Piece O' Cake in 1994, and Becky knows she could not have asked for a better partner.

The two still work together, but Becky has written this book on her own. Color is something she has spent many years thinking about, learning about, and teaching. It feels like the right time for her to put it all in a book.

Designing and making quilts, writing books, and teaching others how to make quilts is a better career than Becky could ever have imagined. Quilters are wonderful people, and she loves being a part of the global quilt world.

You can find Becky online at pieceocake.com.

Online Color Resources

A vast array of color information is available online. Here are a few fun sites to get you started.

Beverly Ash Gilbert beverlyashgilbert.com

Color Matters colormatters.com

Colors on the Web colorsontheweb.com

Colour Code colourco.de

Design Seeds design-seeds.com

Paletton, Color Scheme Designer paletton.com

Also ...

- Just for fun, do an Internet image search for "Vogue Chart Rainbow Queen." It will make you smile.

- iPad App: Interaction of Color by Josef Albers. It's not free, but it is amazing.

Other books by the author:

Available as eBook only

Available as Print-On-Demand and as eBook

Available as Print-On-Demand only

Available as Print-On-Demand only

Available as Print-On-Demand only

Available as Print-On-Demand only

Available as eBook only

Great Titles *from* C&T PUBLISHING

Available at your local retailer or **ctpub.com** *or* **800-284-1114**

For a list of other fine books from C&T Publishing, visit our website to view our catalog online.

C&T PUBLISHING, INC.
P.O. Box 1456
Lafayette, CA 94549
800-284-1114

Email: ctinfo@ctpub.com
Website: ctpub.com

Tips and Techniques can be found at ctpub.com/quilting-sewing-tips.

For quilting supplies:

COTTON PATCH
1025 Brown Ave.
Lafayette, CA 94549
Store: 925-284-1177
Mail order: 925-283-7883

Email: CottonPa@aol.com
Website: quiltusa.com

Note: Fabrics shown may not be currently available, as fabric manufacturers keep most fabrics in print for only a short time.